PEELING THE WILD ONION

A COLLECTION OF CHICAGO CULINARY CULTURE

PEELING THE WILD ONION

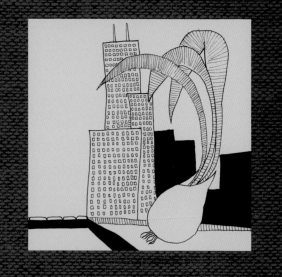

A COLLECTION OF CHICAGO CULINARY CULTURE

FROM THE JUNIOR LEAGUE OF CHICAGO

PEELING THE WILD ONION

A COLLECTION OF CHICAGO CULINARY CULTURE

Published by the Junior League of Chicago
1447 North Astor Street
Chicago, IL 60610
www.jlchicago.org
312-664-4462
312-664-1963 (fax)

Artist: Anne Hankey

This cookbook is a collection of favorite recipes,
which are not necessarily original recipes.

Library of Congress Control Number: 2007930191
ISBN: 978-0-9611622-5-2

Edited, Designed, and Manufactured by
Favorite Recipes® Press
An imprint of

FRP.

P. O. Box 305142
Nashville, Tennessee 37230
800-358-0560

Art Director: Steve Newman
Book Design: Brad Whitfield and Susan Breining
Project Editor: Nicki Pendleton Wood

Manufactured in China
First Printing: 2008   12,500 copies

Mission Statement

The Junior League of Chicago, Inc., is a metropolitan organization of women
committed to promoting voluntarism, developing the potential of women,
and improving the community through effective action and leadership of trained volunteers.
The Junior League of Chicago, Inc., reaches out to women of all races, religions,
and national origins who demonstrate an interest in and a commitment to voluntarism.

Focus Statement

The Junior League of Chicago empowers at-risk families,
especially women and girls,
through mentoring, advocacy, and education.

A Sampling of JLC Community Projects

Project C.A.R.E. • Child Life Assistants • Done in a Day • Homework Heroes
Journey to Independent Living • Learning to Fly • Mad Hatter's Children's Theater Project
Next Step for Teen Moms • Partners Educating Parents • Project CON:CERN
Teen Exodus • The Women's Treatment Center • Woman-to-Woman/North Suburban

2007–2008 Board of Directors

Cookbook Development Team

2005-2006
Board of Directors

Elizabeth Hurley
Michelle Kerr
Linda Lumpkin
Anna Musci
Deborah Hagman-Shannon
Elizabeth Vastine
Michelle Miller Burns
Regina Wootton
Betsy Sproul
Anna Lovis
Norma Weir
Linda Beck
Margaret Smith Palmer
Allison Szafranski

2006-2007
Board of Directors

Michelle Kerr
Ellen Baker
Rae Stapleton
Jennifer Cavanaugh
Julie Pfeiffer
Elizabeth Vastine
Regina Wootton
Laura Anderson
Jana Smith
Joy Valdez
Margaret Lawlis
Linda Beck
Julie Mann

Administrative Director

Ann Brinkman

2006-2007 Cookbook Committee Members

Co-Chairs
Helen Grace Caldwell
Christine T. Foushee

Corporate Sponsorship
Teresa Carpenter
Robin Fisher
Amy Giefers
Katherine Kamp
Erin Walsh

Recipe Organization Chair
Emily Casey

Copy Editing
Maggie Gillette
Lynmarie Lane
Kelly O'Malley
Erin Johnson Remotigue

Recipe Layout
Renata Sutter

Recipe Testing
Amy Baker
Crosby Burke
Cristin Carter
Kathleen Coates
Claire Dwyer
Kelsey Gilreath
Stephanie Krebs
Carolyn Metnick
Christine Orsini Mickey
Irene Morse
Claudia Prieto
Meghanne Sennott
Claudine Tambuatco
Cassie Veatch

Soupcon II Reprint
Katie Cardwell
DeShawna Curtis
Kelly Gilroy
Rachel Ingle
Lauren Pire

Recipe Solicitation
Cathy Cooper
Angela Ferry-Miller
Liza Michaels
Jennifer Risher

Tips and Sidebars
Meredith Benson
Katie Demetriou
Michelle Germann
Meredyth Poulsen
Katie Rice
Claudine Tambuatco
Sara Taylor
Nicolina Traverso
Elizabeth Vadas

Artist
Pen and ink illustrations provided by Anne Hankey, member of the Junior League of Chicago and a local artist

2007-2008 Cookbook Committee Members

Co-Chairs
Helen Grace Caldwell
Kristin Zimmer Shea

Marketing
Katie Anetsberger
Sarah Back
Crosby Burke
Jennifer Cook
Catherine Cooper
JoDee Davis
Shelley Davis

Lisa Diehlman
Angela Disalvo
Claire Dwyer
Robin Fisher
Michelle Germann
Margaret Gillette
Kelly Gilroy
Katy Hester
Ami Hindia
Katherine Kamp
Lynmarie Lane
Cathleen McCann
Kristen Nedoma

Meredyth Poulsen
Jennifer Risher
Elizabeth Ryll
Meghanne Sennott
Susan Speicher
Cluadine Tambuatco
Sara Taylor
Nicolina Traverso
Madeleine Tullier
Cassie Veatch
Juli Villacorta
Hunter Weinberg

Special Thanks

Recipe Testers

Cecilia Abbott
Amy Antochow
Ellen Baker
Habby Bauer
Linda Beck
Melissa Bennis
Meredith Benson
Heidi Betz
Chrissie Bonaguidi
Christina Brunt
Mindi Buckley
Glori Ann Byrd
Helen Grace Caldwell
Rebecca Cook
Kristen Chun
Katie Demetriou
Elizabeth Egen
Brooke Eisenmenger
Erin Fech
Robin Fisher
Christine T. Foushee
Mary S. Foushee
Carolyn Gan
Megan Gemp
Lisa Geyer
Maggie Gillette
Charity Haines
Megan Hanrahan
Natalie Harrison
Liz Hood
Kathleen Iues

Ruth Kelfer
Jennifer King
Wheatley Marshall
Cathleen McCann
Liza Michaels
Ann Oltmann
Kelly O'Malley
Jennifer Perucca
Julie Pfeiffer
Claire Quish
Amy Richards
Jennifer Risher
Annette Nikolich Ryks
Pinsuda Sagoleein
Robin Saunders
Missy Shinall
Molly Shoup
Carolyn Singer
Amy Sproull
Rae Stapleton
Kate Streit
Lindsay Suthard
Dana M Ugolini
Juliana Villacorta
Erin Walsh
Lesley Weber
Michelle Welsh
Elizabeth Whitlow
Suzanne Wilcox
Catherine Wilson
Allyn Wise
Tery Wong

Elizabeth Hurley

Elizabeth Hurley was a champion of this cookbook long before anyone on the committee was hard at work. Everyone who has labored in the development of this project joins in a group "thank you" for her guidance, inspiration, and wit. Thanks, Elizabeth, for your can-do attitude and encouragement every step of the way. Look for this icon next to her recipes. Enjoy her submissions!

Recipe Contributors

Patti Rudin Albaugh
Kathryn Alcock
Jill Anderson
Amy Antochow
Amy Baker
Ellen Baker
Katarzyna Baradziej-Quino
Habby Bauer
Nicole Bell
Meredith Benson
Janis Berlin
Paul Bodine
Chris Bosas
Vern Broder
Recca Brooks
Tami Brooks
Barbara Buck
Barbara Buckham
Kay Buckham
Crosby Burke
Kimberly Burt
Grace Butler
Glori Ann Byrd
Helen Grace Caldwell
Katie Cardwell
Mary Sarah Carpenter
Colleen Carroll
Cristin Carter
Emily Casey
Kathy Coates
Evelyn Cohen
Rebecca Cook
Cathy Cooper
Donna Cooper

Nora Corpuz
Mary Jo Coughlin
Sima Dahl
Erin Daly
Susan Darragh
Samaika DeBose
Eliza Desch
Carla DiGiovanni
Sara Drew
Claire Dwyer
Stephanie Ellis
Alla Feldman
Robin Fisher
Terry Flotken
Ermaline Ford
Roger Fournier
Christine T. Foushee
Mary S. Foushee
Marie Fowler
Stephanie Freeman
Diana Gilroy
Kelly Gilroy
Julia Goalby
Jennifer Gordon
Bernard Graf
Ellen Spicuzza Gull
Emily Hadley
Nicole Halloran
Cindy Hammes
Heidi Holt
Lisa Hong
Elizabeth Hurley
Mark Hurley
Corey Jackier
Leslie Johnson

Linda Johnson
Michael Johnson
Diana Kamp
Olga Kapustina
Ed Kearns
Jason Kearns
Kathy Kelly
Jennifer Kernan
Jeff Kerr
Kate Kinne
Holly Kopec
Keith Krause
Stephanie Krebs
Lynmarie Lane
Amber Larue
Nancy Leavic
Mary Leyden
Hope Lloyd
Anne Logue
Tiffiny Magnus
John & Leslie Mallman
Shilpa Marano
Beth Marrion
Rachel McCall
Cathleen McCann
Jennifer McCormick
Mary McKeon
Ange Dyer McLaughlin
Tiffiniy McTurnan
Jennifer Meisner
Melanie Melaragno
Carolyn Metnick
Liza Michaels
Sandra Michelau
Christine Orsini Mickey

Dorothy Mickey
Margaret Graf Mickey
Angela Ferry Miller
Erminia Miola
Irene Morse
Jeff Muench
Barb Nemeckay
Sandi Newman
Linda Olbeira
Mara O'Brien
Rey Olbeira
Kelly O'Malley
Violet O'Malley
Jan Orlando
Allison Paoli
Joann Pazen
Kelly Pedone
Shon Peebles
Jennifer Perucca
Karen Pickford
Charlotte Pilarski
Mylene Pollock
Christine Pond
Jennifer Pozzouli
Clare Quich
Jennifer Reichers
Erin Johnson Remotigue
Jeffrey Remotigue
Jennifer Risher
Alice Roe
Joanna Roth
Louise Ruffner
Kate Ryan
Annette Nikolich Ryks

Shannon Saunders
Jean Sekera
Sally Seyfarth
Kristine Sheftel
Molly Shoup
Vernata Simon
Kelly Smith
Tim Snyder
Rae Stapleton
Ellen Struck
Sandra Sumner
Lindsay Suthard
Renata Sutter
Margaret Swearengen
Claudine Tambuatco
Karen Terry
Lisa Totino
Bonnie Tromba
Dana Ugolini
Jane Ugolini
Caryn Umbenhauer
Cassie Veatch
Mercedes Vega
Norell Waltmire
Emily Ward
Brandsford Whitlow
Robin Whitre
Denell Whittingham
Amy Wilson
Pat Wood
Kathryn Yerger
Kate York
Lindsey Young
Jennifer Zanowski

Special Thanks

The Junior League of Chicago expresses its sincere and deep appreciation for
the financial support of the following donors.

Sponsors

Harley-Davidson
Financial Services

mary james

the styles of forever

Freeborn & Peters LLP

Attorneys at Law

URBAN SEARCH
REAL ESTATE
(312) 337-2400

The Spice House

Four Corners

Southport Grocery

Patrons

Chase Investments on behalf
of Helen G. Caldwell

Whole Foods Market

Brighton Corporation

Spirit Walker 28380

The Cardwell Family

Irene F. Morse

Erin Walsh

Rachel Ingle

Entendré Boutique

Friends of Crosby Burke

Zoran Raskovich

City Smiles

Motorola on behalf of
Michelle Germann

Table of Contents

Introduction   12

Spring 13

Menus 16

Summer 49

Menus 52

Table of Contents

Fall 97

Menus 100

Winter 129

Menus 132

Introduction

Every grade school student in Chicago learns that the word *Chicago* comes from the Pottawatomie word for "wild onion." While this historical fact may seem trivial, it is significant and even prophetic. A food tour through Chicago reveals world-renowned gastronomic destinations, ethnic eateries tucked away in quiet neighborhoods, hot dog stands dotting the landscape, chaotic wholesale food hubs, and blossoming farmers' markets. True to its name, Chicago is all about food.

Recently, the national and international press have turned their attention to Chicago, hailing it as a great food city and epicenter of some of the most cutting-edge dining in the country. While Chicagoans don't mind the positive press, it's really no surprise to us. Chicago is built on a long tradition of innovative dining establishments and food manufacturing industry.

In the minds of many, Chicago is famous for its meat industry and most specifically the historical stockyards. While the stockyards have faded away, Chicago remains a powerhouse of meat processing and sausage making. Along the way, this meat-centric focus gave rise to Italian beef, our own unique hot dog, and numerous steakhouses.

The baking and candy industries are another pillar of Chicago's food manufacturing industry. Chicago was home to the first fully automated bread factory in 1910 and birthplace of the Twinkie, the Tootsie Roll, O'Henry and Baby Ruth candy bars, Frango Mints, and Cracker Jack.

CHRISTOPHER KOETKE
Dean
The School of Culinary Arts in Kendall College

Through the decades, visionary chefs and restaurateurs shaped not only the Chicago culinary culture, but also eating habits across the United States. Chicago has a plausible claim to the first cafeteria, which opened in the 1890s. In the 1960s, Rich Melman of Lettuce Entertain You fame pioneered the salad bar, changing food service for several decades. Chicago is also home to many now-famous dishes created in restaurant and hotel kitchens. The Palmer House is credited with cooking the first chocolate brownie in 1893. The Hotel de Jonge invented Shrimp de Jonge, and Chicken Vesuvio was reportedly created in Chicago. In the late 1960s, Saganaki was Americanized in our Greek Town with the addition of flaming alcohol. Another hometown favorite, deep-dish pizza, challenged the rest of the country to broaden its definition of pizza. Chicago is also known as a center for culinary education, and since 1937, home to the longest-operating culinary school, Washburne Trade School. Here at Kendall College, we prepare the next generation of leaders in the food service and hospitality industries. Our students study culinary history to better interpret current culinary evolution. We also recognize the importance of the great culinary diversity concentrated in our city as an inspiration for culinary creation.

This fifth edition of the Chicago Junior League cookbook also reflects Chicago's rich history and diversity concentrated in our city as an inspiration for culinary creation. Producing a Junior League cookbook is a labor of love that supports the benevolent work of the Junior League and continues a tradition dating from 1943. The edition now joins the ranks of more than two hundred other Junior League cookbooks currently in print and will represent our food-centric city, the wild onion, proudly. I invite you to peel back the pages of this wild onion and discover the treasures within.

SPRING

Spring for Chicagoans means thawing out with long walks on the beach and romps with the dog.

As each day grows longer, the city becomes more awake and active—from Saint Patrick's Day when the Chicago River

runs a vivid Irish green to the first pitch from the Cubs at Wrigley Field or the White Sox at Cellular Field.

The new season means street fairs, shopping, and jogging in the park as we enjoy the spirit of renewal and growth.

And while spring has a later start here than in other Midwest cities, flip-flops and budding tulips

are a sure sign that no matter how late, spring has arrived!

SPRING

SPRING MENUS

MOTHER'S DAY BRUNCH

Back-in-the-South Mint Julep, 17

Mushroom and Swiss Quiche, 19

Vegetable and Cheese Strata, 20

Asparagus in Hazelnut Butter, 42

Chicken Prosciutto Rolls, 33

Hot Herb Bread, 20

Lemon Tea Bread, 21

QUEEN FOR A DAY

Rise and shine with our Mother's Day Brunch fit for a queen. Afterwards, give your mom the royal treatment with these sure-to-please activities. Whether you indulge in one or splurge for all four, these activities will be time well-spent together—the best gift of all.

Relax with spa-tacular treatments at The Peninsula Hotel.

Enjoy a "spot" of tea at the Drake Hotel.

Window shop on Oak Street and the Magnificent Mile.

Sip martinis atop the city at the Hancock Building's Signature Lounge.

GET A JUMP ON SUMMER GRILLING

Bourbon Slush, 17

Lemon Basil Grilled Pork Chops, 36

Grilled Salmon with
Cucumber Melon Salsa, 40

Garlic Rosemary Flatbread, 24

Roasted Spring Vegetables, 42

Lemon Bars, 45

Ahh . . . spring in Chicago! Flip-flops, porches, and grills! We may not have spacious backyards, but that doesn't mean we don't make room—no matter how small the outdoor space—for our beloved grills. Use the first day of the welcomed warm weather to fire up the "old faithful," treat your neighbors to the scents of grilled pork or salmon, and toast your first outdoor meal with a fine Bourbon Slush.

CINCO DE MAYO SUPPER

Black Bean and Goat Cheese
Quesadillas, 25

Asparagus Guacamole, 25

Roast Pork with Mole Sauce, 37

Mexican Rice, 43

Key Lime Cake, 47

Mango and Lime Ice, 47

With the third largest population of Mexican immigrants in the United States, Chicago has a proud Mexican heritage and annually celebrates the victory of the Mexican militia over the French army at the Battle of Puebla in 1862 with live music, food vendors, carnival rides, and a parade in Douglas Park. The parade is a colorful procession that begins at the intersection of Cermak Road and Damen Avenue and heads west to Marshall Boulevard. A replica of the Virgin of Guadalupe serves as the grand marshal. After enjoying the festivities at Douglas Park, bring a little celebration home with you by serving some of our favorite Hispanic dishes.

The party doesn't stop on May 6. Many Mexican merchants gather on Sundays at the Maxwell Street Market. Open since 1912, the market is visited by as many as 20,000 people on an average day.

Bourbon Slush

1 (12-ounce) can frozen lemonade
concentrate, thawed
1 (6-ounce) can frozen orange juice
concentrate, thawed
1 cup sugar
6 cups water
1¹/₂ cups bourbon
2 cups brewed tea

Combine the lemonade concentrate, orange juice concentrate, sugar, water, bourbon and tea in a large plastic container or sealable plastic bag and mix well. Freeze for 6 to 8 hours or until slushy. Stir or break the mixture apart and freeze for an additional 24 hours.

Serve in frosted glasses.

Yield: 8 to 10 servings

Back-in-the-South Mint Julep

²/₃ cup sugar
¹/₃ cup water
3 bunches mint, roughly torn and bruised
1 fifth of bourbon
2 tablespoons vanilla extract
Sprigs of fresh mint (optional)

Combine the sugar, water and 2 bunches of the mint in a large saucepan. Bring to a boil and simmer until the sugar is completely dissolved. Cool thoroughly. Strain into a large bowl and discard the mint. Stir in the bourbon and vanilla. Stuff the empty bourbon bottle with the remaining 1 bunch mint. Pour the bourbon mixture back into the bottle. Freeze for 8 to 10 hours. Pour over crushed ice in silver julep cups and garnish with sprigs of mint.

Yield: 8 to 10 servings

French Toast Kabob

This recipe was provided by the Executive Chef of Orange.

12 eggs, beaten with 2 tablespoons water
1¹/₂ cups coconut milk
1 loaf *pain de mie* or (crustless) white bread,
cut into 1-inch slices
1 pineapple, trimmed and sliced into 1-inch rings
1 pint strawberries, trimmed

Whisk the scrambled egg mixture and coconut milk together in a large bowl. Dip the bread slices in the egg mixture and squeeze gently in the liquid to soak the bread. Place the slices on a greased baking sheet. Bake in a preheated 350-degree oven for 10 to 15 minutes or until golden brown. Cool completely. Grill the pineapple rings over medium heat until tender. Cool completely.

Cut half of the coconut toasts into 3×3-inch squares. Cut the pineapple rings into quarters, discarding the tough center part. Soak bamboo skewers in water; pat dry. Thread the coconut toast squares, pineapple pieces and strawberries on the skewers, beginning and ending with the coconut toast. Arrange the skewers and remaining whole coconut bread slices on a baking sheet. Bake in a preheated 350-degree oven for 5 to 10 minutes or just until reheated.

To serve, slice the coconut toasts in half. Stack two halves on each plate and stack 1 or 2 kabob skewers on top. Serve with your favorite fruit dipping sauce and/or maple syrup.

Yield: 12 servings

TIP: *Pain de mie* is a type of sliced, packaged white bread.
Pain in French means "loaf of bread," and *mie* means "crumb." In English this is
most like a "pullman loaf" or regular sandwich bread with crusts removed.

Mushroom and Swiss Quiche

1 unbaked (9-inch) pie shell
2 eggs
1 tablespoon all-purpose flour
8 slices bacon, crisp-cooked and crumbled
4$^{1}/_{2}$ ounces sliced mushrooms
1$^{1}/_{2}$ cups (6 ounces) shredded Swiss cheese
1 onion, chopped
1 cup evaporated milk
$^{1}/_{2}$ teaspoon salt
$^{1}/_{4}$ teaspoon garlic powder
Dash of hot red pepper sauce
Dash of dry mustard
Dash of nutmeg

Bake the pie shell in a preheated 400-degree oven for 5 minutes or until golden brown. Beat the eggs and flour together in a large bowl. Stir in the bacon, mushrooms, cheese, onion, evaporated milk, salt, garlic powder, hot red pepper sauce, dry mustard and nutmeg. Pour into the baked pie shell. Bake in a preheated 350-degree oven for 45 minutes or until a knife inserted in the center comes out clean.

Yield: 6 servings

BAKE A PERFECT QUICHE

To test whether the quiche is done, watch the oven, not the clock. Look for a light golden brown coloring on the surface of the quiche, which may puff up slightly as it bakes. A knife blade inserted about an inch from the edge should come out clean; the center may still be slightly liquid, but internal heat will finish the baking and the filling will solidify as it cools. Be sure to set the baked quiche on a wire rack to cool so that air circulates around it.

Vegetable and Cheese Strata

This recipe requires overnight refrigeration.

1 teaspoon olive oil
2 cups diced zucchini
2 cups sliced mushrooms
1 cup diced red bell pepper
1 cup diced onion
2 garlic cloves, crushed
3/4 cup chopped canned artichoke hearts
8 cups (1-inch) cubed Italian bread
1 cup (4 ounces) shredded extra-sharp Cheddar cheese
1/4 cup freshly grated Parmesan cheese
6 eggs or 1 1/2 cups egg substitute
1 (12-ounce) can evaporated milk
1 teaspoon Italian seasoning
1/2 teaspoon dry mustard
1/4 teaspoon salt
1/4 teaspoon pepper
Sprigs of oregano (optional)

Heat the olive oil in a nonstick skillet over medium-high heat. Add the zucchini, mushrooms, bell pepper, onion and garlic. Sauté for 6 minutes or until tender. Remove from the heat and stir in the artichoke hearts. Arrange the bread cubes in a 9×13-inch baking dish. Spoon the zucchini mixture evenly over the bread cubes. Sprinkle with the cheeses. Whisk the egg substitute, evaporated milk, Italian seasoning, mustard, salt and pepper together in a bowl. Pour over the cheese layer. Chill, covered with foil. Bake in a preheated 325-degree oven for 1 hour or until bubbly. Let stand for 30 minutes before serving. Garnish with sprigs of oregano.

Yield: 8 servings

TIP: Sauté vegetables to remove excess moisture and prevent the casserole from becoming waterlogged.

Hot Herb Bread

1/2 cup (1 stick) butter, softened
1 teaspoon parsley flakes
1/4 teaspoon oregano
1/4 teaspoon dill weed
1/8 teaspoon garlic powder
Grated Parmesan cheese to taste
1 loaf French bread, cut diagonally into 1-inch slices
Additional Parmesan cheese
Additional parsley flakes

Combine the butter, 1 teaspoon parsley flakes, the oregano, dill weed, garlic powder and Parmesan cheese to taste in a small bowl and mix well. Spread on both sides of the bread slices. Reassemble the loaf on a sheet of foil and shape the foil around the loaf, twisting the ends and leaving the top open. Sprinkle with additional Parmesan cheese and parsley flakes. Bake in a preheated 400-degree oven for 10 minutes.

Yield: 8 to 10 servings

Lemon Tea Bread

6 tablespoons butter, softened
1 1/4 cups sugar
2 eggs, beaten
1/2 teaspoon lemon extract
1 1/2 cups plus 1 tablespoon all-purpose flour
1 teaspoon baking powder
1/4 teaspoon salt
1/2 cup milk
Grated lemon zest
Dash of ground cloves
Juice of 1 lemon
1/4 cup sugar

Cream the butter and 1 1/4 cups sugar in a mixing bowl until light and fluffy. Beat in the eggs and lemon extract. Sift the flour, baking powder and salt together. Add to the creamed mixture alternately with the milk, mixing well after each addition. Stir in the lemon zest and cloves. Pour into a greased and floured 5x9-inch loaf pan. Bake in a preheated 350-degree oven for 1 hour or until the bread tests done. Combine the lemon juice and 1/4 cup sugar in a small bowl and mix well. Pour over the hot bread. Cool in the pan for 15 minutes. Remove to a wire rack to cool completely.

Yield: 8 servings

COOKING IRISH-STYLE

Brush up on your Irish cooking terms with this food glossary:

COLCANNON—made of potato and wild garlic, cabbage or curly kale, butter, salt, and pepper. The dish may contain other ingredients such as milk, cream, leeks, onions, or chives. This is an inexpensive, year-round staple food. An Irish Halloween tradition is to serve small coins concealed in colcannon.

CHAMP (aka poundies)— mashed potatoes mixed with chopped scallions.

BOXTY—an Irish potato pancake that has a uniquely smooth, fine-grained consistency.

CODDLE— layers of pork sausage and streaky rashers (bacon) with sliced potatoes and onions boiled in liquid. Salt, pepper, and parsley are the usual flavorings. Coddle is traditionally accompanied by a pint of Guinness.

FARLS—a type of flatbread, cooked on a griddle and unique to Northern Ireland. This potato bread, also known as fadge, slims, potato cake, or potato farls, is a form of unleavened bread in which potato replaces a major portion of the regular wheat flour.

Irish Soda Bread

3 cups all-purpose flour
1/3 cup sugar
1 tablespoon baking powder
1 teaspoon baking soda
2 cups buttermilk
1 egg, lightly beaten
1/4 cup (1/2 stick) butter, melted

Combine the flour, sugar, baking powder and baking soda in a large bowl. Whisk the buttermilk and egg together in a bowl. Add to the dry ingredients and stir just until mixed. Stir in the melted butter. Pour into a greased 5x9-inch loaf pan. Bake in a preheated 325-degree oven for 60 to 65 minutes or until a wooden pick inserted in the center comes out clean. Remove from the pan to a wire rack to cool. Wrap in plastic wrap and store for 8 hours before slicing.

Yield: 8 to 10 servings

TIP: For individual loaves, use miniature loaf pans and reduce the baking time accordingly.

Pierogi

DOUGH
5 cups unbleached all-purpose flour
1 egg
Salt to taste
1 tablespoon canola oil
1 1/2 cups water, boiled then cooled

FILLING
Sauerkraut and Mushroom Filling (at right)
Meat and Mushroom Filling (page 23)
Potato and Cheese Filling (page 23)
Blueberry or Strawberry Filling (page 23)

For the dough, measure the flour into a large mixing bowl and make a well in the center. Beat the egg with a little salt. Pour into the flour and stir with a wooden spoon. Add the oil and enough of the water gradually to make a soft dough, stirring constantly. Knead on a floured surface until elastic and a little sticky. Let stand, covered with the bowl, for 20 minutes.

For the filling and assembly, roll a portion of the dough 1/8 inch thick on a floured surface, keeping the remaining dough covered. Cut into circles with a cookie cutter or glass. Place 1 to 2 teaspoons of the desired filling in the center of each circle. Moisten the edges with water; fold the edges together to form a half-circle and crimp to seal. Repeat the process with the remaining dough. Bring a large pot of salted water to a boil and reduce the heat to medium. Lower the pierogi 12 at a time into the water. Simmer for 3 to 5 minutes, timing from the moment they float to the top; drain.

Serve immediately.

Yield: 24 servings

Kapusta (Sauerkraut and Mushroom Filling)

Fresh sauerkraut, dried wild mushrooms, and Maggi seasoning can be found in Polish stores or local delis.

1 cup dried wild mushrooms
1 pound fresh sauerkraut, rinsed well
2 onions, cut into 1/4-inch slices
4 tablespoons canola oil
Salt and pepper to taste
Maggi or Vegeta seasoning to taste

Soak the mushrooms in cold water to cover for several hours. Boil the mushrooms in the same water in a saucepan for 30 minutes; drain. Simmer the sauerkraut in water to cover in a saucepan for 20 to 30 minutes; let cool and drain well.

Process the mushrooms and sauerkraut in a meat grinder or food processor just until finely chopped. Sauté the onions in the canola oil in a skillet until tender and golden. Stir in the mushroom mixture and enough water to slightly thicken. Add salt, pepper and Maggi seasoning.

Cook over medium heat for 10 minutes, stirring constantly. Cool completely before assembling the pierogi.

Meat and Mushroom Filling

2 onions, cut into $1/4$-inch slices
1 cup sliced mushrooms
Vegetable oil for sautéing
1 pound ground beef or veal
Salt and pepper to taste
Maggi or Vegeta seasoning to taste

Sauté the onions and mushrooms in a small amount of oil in a skillet until tender and golden. Remove to a food processor and pulse for 10 seconds or just until finely chopped. Brown the ground beef in a skillet, stirring until crumbly; drain. Stir in the onion mixture and sauté for 3 minutes. Add salt, pepper and Maggi seasoning. Cool completely.

PULASKI DAY

Chicago celebrates honored Polish Commander Casimir Pulaski on the first Monday in March. The celebration kicks off with an annual parade, well attended because schools around the city and throughout Illinois are closed. The day off offers the opportunity to visit the Polish Museum of America—one of the oldest and largest ethnic museums in the United States!

Potato and Cheese Filling

2 onions, cut into $1/4$-inch slices
1 tablespoon canola oil
1 pound Idaho potatoes, peeled, cooked and mashed by hand
8 ounces farmer cheese, mashed
Salt and pepper to taste
Sour cream (optional)

Sauté the onions in the canola oil in a skillet until tender and golden. Add the potatoes, cheese, salt and pepper and mix well. Cool completely. Serve sour cream with these pierogi.

Blueberry or Strawberry Filling

1 pound blueberries or strawberries, cut into $1/4$-inch slices
Sugar to taste

Sprinkle the blueberries or strawberries with a little sugar.

Serve fruit-filled pierogi with vanilla sauce: whip heavy whipping cream with a little sugar, a few drops of vanilla extract, and lemon juice. This is a great dessert for kids.

Garlic Rosemary Flatbread

1 pound pizza dough, at room temperature
1 tablespoon unsalted butter
1 tablespoon extra-virgin olive oil
1 garlic clove, minced
1 teaspoon kosher salt
1/2 teaspoon finely chopped fresh rosemary
Cornmeal for sprinkling
Sprigs of rosemary (optional)

Spread the pizza dough thinly on an ungreased baking sheet. Melt the butter with the olive oil in a small saucepan. Brush over the dough. Sprinkle the garlic, salt and rosemary evenly over the top. Bake in a preheated 400-degree oven until browned. Sprinkle with cornmeal and cut into pieces. Garnish with sprigs of rosemary.

Yield: 4 servings

TIP: Be sure to roll the dough quite thin to yield the crackerlike texture that's traditional in these Scandinavian crisps.

Pear and Ginger Muffins

1 3/4 cups all-purpose flour
1/2 cup packed light brown sugar
3/4 cup granulated sugar
2 teaspoons baking powder
1 teaspoon ground ginger
2/3 cup sour cream
1/2 cup vegetable oil
2 tablespoons honey
2 eggs
1 1/2 cups peeled, cored and finely chopped
  (1/4-inch) pears
1/4 cup packed light brown sugar

Combine the flour, 1/2 cup brown sugar, the granulated sugar, baking powder and ginger in a bowl and mix well. Whisk the sour cream, oil, honey and eggs together in a bowl. Str in the dry ingredients just until moistened. Fold in the pears. Pour into 12 paper-lined muffin cups. Sprinkle 1/4 cup brown sugar evenly over the muffins. Bake in a preheated 375-degree oven for 20 minutes or until firm to the touch. Remove to a wire rack.

Serve the muffins while still warm.

Yield: 12 servings

Black Bean and Goat Cheese Quesadillas

1 cup chopped onion
2 garlic cloves, minced
1 teaspoon virgin olive oil
1 (19-ounce) can black beans
$1/2$ cup salsa
$1/4$ teaspoon cumin
6 ounces goat cheese, crumbled
$1/3$ cup minced fresh cilantro
8 (8-inch) flour tortillas
1 teaspoon extra-virgin olive oil
$1/2$ cup sour cream
$1/2$ cup salsa

Sauté the onion and garlic in 1 teaspoon olive oil in a large skillet over medium-high heat for 3 minutes. Stir in the undrained beans, $1/2$ cup salsa and the cumin. Bring to a boil. Reduce the heat and simmer for 5 minutes or until thick. Mash the bean mixture slightly with a potato masher. Remove from the heat and stir in the goat cheese and cilantro. Spread 4 tortillas with the bean mixture. Top each with 1 of the remaining tortillas and press gently. Sauté 1 quesadilla in $1/4$ teaspoon olive oil in a skillet over medium-high heat for 2 minutes on each side. Repeat the process with the remaining quesadillas. Cut each quesadilla into six wedges.

Serve with the sour cream and $1/2$ cup salsa.

Yield: 8 servings

Asparagus Guacamole

1 chipotle chile
1 teaspoon extra-virgin olive oil
5 to 8 fresh asparagus spears, trimmed
6 ounces plain yogurt
2 avocados, cubed
1 plum tomato, seeded and diced
1 tablespoon chopped green onion
$1/4$ cup chopped fresh cilantro
1 tablespoon fresh lime juice
$1/2$ teaspoon kosher salt
$1/2$ teaspoon freshly ground pepper
$1/4$ teaspoon minced garlic

Coat the chile with the olive oil and place on a rack in a broiler pan. Broil for 5 minutes or until the chile is charred on all sides, turning frequently. Place in a sealable plastic bag for 10 minutes. Chop the chile finely, discarding the stem, skin and seeds. Fill a sauté pan halfway with water. Bring to a boil. Add the asparagus and simmer for 4 minutes or just until tender. Plunge the spears into a bowl of ice water; drain and dry thoroughly. Cut the spears into quarters. Process the asparagus, yogurt and avocados in a blender or food processor until smooth. Remove to a bowl. Stir in the tomato, green onion, cilantro, lime juice, salt, pepper, garlic and chile one ingredient at a time and in the order listed.

Yield: 6 to 8 servings

TIP: When storing guacamole, place plastic wrap directly on the surface to prevent discoloration.

Roasted Pepper and Walnut Dip

4 red bell peppers (about 2 pounds),
seeded and cut in half lengthwise
1 cup chopped onion
1/2 cup chopped walnuts
3 garlic cloves, minced
1 tablespoon cumin
1/8 teaspoon ground red pepper
1 teaspoon honey
1/2 teaspoon salt
9 (6-inch) pita or flatbread rounds,
each cut into 8 wedges

Place the pepper halves skin side up on a foil-lined baking sheet and flatten gently. Broil for 12 minutes or until blackened. Set aside. Peel the peppers and process them in a food processor until smooth. Place in a large greased skillet over medium-high heat. Add the onion, walnuts, garlic, cumin and ground red pepper and sauté for 8 minutes. Stir in the bell pepper purée, honey and salt. Cook for 5 minutes longer. Cool completely. Process in a food processor until smooth. Chill, covered, until serving time.

Serve with the pita wedges.

Yield: 18 appetizer servings

Gourmet Pecans

1 cup sugar
1/2 teaspoon salt
1 egg white
3 tablespoons Kahlúa
4 cups (or more) small pecan halves

Mix the sugar and salt in a small bowl. Whisk the egg white and Kahlúa together in a large bowl. Add the pecans and stir to coat well. Add the sugar mixture and stir well. Spread the pecans in a single layer on a foil-lined 10×15-inch baking pan. Bake in a preheated 325-degree oven for 20 to 25 minutes or until toasted and crisp, stirring every 10 minutes. Remove the pecans immediately from the foil. Cool on waxed paper.

Yield: 4 cups

Brie and Walnut Cake

This recipe requires overnight refrigeration.

15 ounces goat cheese
4 ounces mild blue cheese
1 medium wheel Brie cheese, chilled
1 cup walnut halves, toasted and chopped
1 cup ruby port
$^1/_4$ cup honey
2 sprigs of fresh thyme
1 cup seedless red grapes, sliced into $^1/_4$-inch pieces
Additional walnut halves, toasted (optional)
Sprigs of thyme (optional)

Cream the goat cheese and blue cheese in a bowl until soft and smooth. Slice the Brie wheel in half horizontally and gently ease the two halves apart. Spread $^3/_4$ cup of the goat cheese mixture over one half of the Brie. Sprinkle with 1 cup walnuts. Top with the remaining Brie half cut side down. Spread the remaining goat cheese mixture over the top of the Brie. Chill for 2 hours or overnight. Combine the port, honey and 2 sprigs thyme in a small saucepan. Bring to a boil over medium-high heat and simmer for 6 minutes or until reduced by half. Add the grapes. Cook for 30 seconds longer. Remove the grapes to a bowl, using a slotted spoon. Simmer the remaining liquid for 6 minutes or until thickened. Remove and discard the thyme sprigs.

Place the Brie cake on a serving platter and top with the grapes. Drizzle with the port syrup. Garnish with walnut halves and sprigs of thyme.

Yield: 8 servings

TIP: Don't have cheese wire? Use unflavored dental floss in place of cheese wire to slice the Brie in half.

Grilled Antipasto Vegetables

This recipe requires overnight refrigeration.

6 garlic cloves, crushed
1 tablespoon chopped serrano chile
3/4 teaspoon salt
3 tablespoons red wine vinegar
2 tablespoons fresh lemon juice
2 tablespoons water
1 1/2 tablespoons extra-virgin olive oil
1 1/2 tablespoons anchovy paste
4 red bell peppers, halved and seeded
4 red onions, each cut into 6 wedges
2 pounds asparagus, trimmed
6 (4-inch) portobello caps
2 teaspoons olive oil

Combine the garlic, serrano chile and salt in a mortar; mash to a paste. Place in a small bowl. Whisk in the vinegar, lemon juice, water, 1 1/2 tablespoons olive oil and the anchovy paste. Store in the refrigerator for up to 1 week.

Grill the bell peppers and onions for 15 minutes or until the peppers are blackened, turning occasionally. Peel and slice the peppers into 1/2-inch strips. Chop the onions into 1-inch pieces. Combine the onions and bell peppers in a large bowl and set aside. Combine the asparagus, portobello caps and 2 teaspoons olive oil in another bowl and toss well. Grill for 3 minutes on each side or until tender. Chop the portobello caps into 1-inch pieces and add to the onion mixture. Slice the asparagus diagonally into 1 1/2-inch pieces and add to the onion mixture. Drizzle the vegetables with the vinaigrette and toss well.

Yield: 11 cups

TIP: This recipe calls for using a mortar and pestle.

Fresh Dill Potato Salad

1 cup plain yogurt
1 cup mayonnaise
1/4 cup diced scallions
1 tablespoon chopped fresh dill weed
2 to 3 pounds potatoes, cooked and cubed
Thinly sliced radishes (optional)

Combine the yogurt, mayonnaise, scallions and dill weed in a large bowl and mix well. Stir in the potatoes. Chill until serving time. Garnish with sliced radishes.

Yield: 4 servings

POTATO TIPS

Try to buy potatoes that are all the same size so that they cook evenly.

Cook potatoes whole in their skins for better flavor and texture. This will also keep them from becoming waterlogged.

Always start potatoes in cold, not boiling, water; otherwise, the outsides will be done before the insides.

Keep the water at a steady simmer. This is a good point to remember when cooking any vegetable; a rolling boil will jostle vegetables, causing them to break apart.

Poppy Seed Chicken Salad

Best when refrigerated overnight before serving.

4 cups cubed cooked chicken
1 cup pecans, toasted and chopped
1 rib celery, cut into 1/4-inch slices
   (about 1 cup)
2 tablespoons finely chopped shallots
2 cups halved seedless red grapes
3/4 cup mayonnaise
2 tablespoons cider vinegar
1 tablespoon honey
1 tablespoon poppy seeds
1/2 teaspoon salt
1/2 teaspoon pepper

Toss the chicken, pecans, celery, shallots, grapes, mayonnaise, vinegar, honey, poppy seeds, salt and pepper together in a large salad bowl. Chill for up to 4 days before serving.

Yield: 4 to 6 servings

Artichoke Soup with Bacon Foam

This recipe was provided by the Executive Chef of NoMi of The Park Hyatt, Chicago.

ARTICHOKE SOUP	BACON FOAM
12 large artichoke hearts, quartered	4 shallots, minced
5 shallots, minced	1 garlic clove
2 garlic cloves	1 bay leaf
1 bay leaf	1 tablespoon vegetable oil
4 sprigs thyme	1/2 bottle white wine
1 tablespoon vegetable oil	2 cups heavy cream
1/2 bottle white wine	1/4 pound uncooked sliced bacon
6 cups vegetable stock	1 1/2 sheets gelatin
2 cups heavy cream	1 teaspoon chopped hazelnuts
	1 pinch of cayenne pepper

For the soup, sauté the artichoke hearts, shallots, garlic, bay leaf and thyme in the oil in a stockpot until the shallots are tender. Pour in the white wine. Simmer to deglaze the pan, stirring constantly. Add the vegetable stock and cream. Simmer for 30 minutes or until the artichoke hearts are tender. Remove and discard the bay leaf and thyme sprigs. Purée the mixture in a blender until smooth. Pass through a fine mesh sieve into a clean stockpot. Keep warm until ready to serve.

For the foam, sauté the shallots, garlic and bay leaf in the oil in a skillet until the shallots are tender. Add the white wine and cream and bring to a simmer. Add the bacon slices and simmer gently for 20 minutes. Cover the pot if necessary to prevent the mixture from reducing. Remove and discard the shallots, garlic, bay leaf and bacon. Soak the gelatin in warm water to cover until softened. Add to the cream mixture and stir until completely dissolved. Pour into an ISI whipping canister and add 2 cartridges. Test to be sure the canister will foam properly. (ISI canisters are available at most culinary stores.)

To serve, pour the soup into warm bowls. Top each serving with 1 teaspoon chopped hazelnuts, a pinch of cayenne pepper and 2 tablespoons of the bacon foam.

Yield: 6 servings

TIP: Professional kitchens use gelatin in sheet form, which produces
a clearer finished product than granular gelatin. Three to four sheets of gelatin
is the equivalent of one envelope of granular gelatin.

The Drake's Cape Cod Bookbinder Red Snapper Soup

This recipe was provided by the Executive Chef of The Drake Hotel.

2 cups sliced celery	1 tablespoon Worcestershire sauce
3 cups chopped carrots	4 bay leaves
1/2 cup chopped red bell pepper	1 tablespoon crushed black
1/2 cup chopped green bell pepper	peppercorns
3 cups chopped onions	1 tablespoon chopped fresh cilantro
1 garlic clove	1 sprig rosemary
3 tablespoons olive oil	Cornstarch
2 cups tomato purée	8 drops caramel color
1/2 cup tomato paste	1 teaspoon garlic salt
12 cups vegetable stock	Kosher salt to taste
3 cups dry cooking sherry	2 pounds red snapper fillets
1 cup dry white wine	3 cups diced white onions
1 tablespoon chicken base	3 ribs celery, thinly sliced

Sauté 2 cups celery, the carrots, bell peppers, 3 cups onions and the garlic in the olive oil in a stockpot until tender. Stir in the tomato purée and tomato paste. Add the vegetable stock, sherry and white wine. Bring to a boil over medium-high heat. Add the chicken base, Worcestershire sauce, bay leaves, peppercorns, cilantro and rosemary. Add cornstarch as needed to thicken the stock. Stir in the caramel color, garlic salt and kosher salt. Simmer for 2 hours. Adjust the seasonings and strain through a China cap. Bake or sauté the red snapper fillets as desired. Flake and add to the stock. Steam the remaining onions and celery and add to the stock.

Yield: 30 cups

TIPS FROM THE DRAKE

The "China cap" is also called a chinois or a bouillon strainer. It's a very fine sieve used mainly to strain sauces, stocks, and puréed soups and is an essential tool in French-style cooking.

A roux is a 1:1 mixture of flour and fat that is used to thicken soups and sauces.
In traditional French cooking, butter is the chosen fat. In Louisiana, vegetable oil or lard is used.
To make a roux, stir the flour and the fat mixture constantly. A butter roux must be cooked over low heat or the butter will burn. The longer the mixture is cooked, the darker the roux becomes and the nuttier the flavor. A light roux is best for thickening; a dark roux is used to add a rich flavor.

"Oak Street" Beach Chicken

4 small boneless skinless chicken breasts
$1/2$ cup all-purpose flour
$1/3$ cup vegetable oil or shortening
1 teaspoon salt
$1/4$ teaspoon pepper
1 (14-ounce) can pineapple slices in juice or syrup
1 cup sugar
2 tablespoons cornstarch
$3/4$ cup cider vinegar
1 cup chicken broth
1 tablespoon soy sauce
$1/4$ teaspoon ground ginger
1 large green bell pepper, cut into rings

Coat the chicken with the flour. Heat the oil in a large skillet. Add the chicken and cook just until browned on both sides. Remove skin side up to a shallow baking pan. Season with salt and pepper. Drain the pineapple liquid into a 2-cup measuring cup. Add enough water to make $1^1/2$ cups. Combine the pineapple liquid with the sugar, cornstarch, vinegar, chicken broth, soy sauce and ginger in a saucepan. Bring to a boil, stirring constantly. Boil for 2 minutes. Pour over the chicken. Bake in a preheated 350-degree oven for 30 minutes. Top with pineapple and bell pepper slices. Bake for 30 minutes longer.

Yield: 4 servings

HOW TO PICK A PINEAPPLE

Once pineapples are picked, they won't become sweeter, although they will become softer. You can tell that a pineapple is ripe if the leaves at the base come off easily when pulled.

Cornish Hens with Whiskey Sauce

6 (1-pound) Cornish game hens
1 garlic clove
1 teaspoon salt
$^1/_4$ teaspoon pepper
$^1/_4$ cup honey
$^1/_4$ cup whiskey
$^1/_2$ cup (1 stick) butter, melted

Place the game hens in a shallow baking pan. Crush the garlic and salt together in a bowl. Add the pepper, honey, whiskey and butter and mix well. Brush some of the mixture over the hens. Bake in a preheated 350-degree oven for 1 to 1$^1/_2$ hours, basting frequently with the remaining whiskey mixture.

Yield: 6 servings

ROASTED POTATOES

Roasted potatoes are a perfect accompaniment to either dish, especially the rack of lamb!

Roast potatoes should be crisp and deep golden brown on the outside, with a moist, velvety, dense interior. Skin should be left intact, providing a contrast with the sweet caramelized flavor that the flesh develops during roasting. Here are some tips.

Use a waxy potato such as Red Bliss, which is better able to retain moisture than baking potatoes.

Covering potatoes with foil causes the potatoes to steam in their own moisture and cuts the cooking time.

Use olive oil, not butter, to rub on the outside of the potatoes. They need to roast at a high temperature (425 degrees) and the butter is likely to burn.

For a garlic flavor, toss the potatoes with raw mashed garlic right after they come out of the oven. The garlic will burn if it roasts along with the potatoes.

Spiced Rack of Lamb

2 racks of lamb
Kosher salt and black pepper to taste
1 teaspoon cayenne pepper
1 teaspoon paprika
1 teaspoon mace
1 teaspoon coriander
2 tablespoons extra-virgin olive oil
Fresh mint leaves (optional)

Season the lamb with kosher salt and black pepper. Combine the cayenne pepper, paprika, mace and coriander in a small bowl and mix well. Rub all over the lamb. Brown the lamb on both sides in the olive oil in a large skillet. Remove to a rack in a roasting pan. Roast in a preheated 425-degree oven for 20 minutes or to 130 degrees (rare) on a meat thermometer. Garnish with fresh mint leaves.

Yield: 4 servings

Ahi Tuna Salad with Asian Vinaigrette

2 pounds ahi tuna, skin removed
2 tablespoons extra-virgin olive oil
Salt and pepper to taste
1 cup thinly sliced red cabbage
1 cup thinly sliced napa cabbage
1/2 cup shredded carrots, blanched
1 avocado, chopped
1/2 red onion, diced
1/4 cup scallions, thinly sliced
Asian Vinaigrette (at right)

Rub the tuna with olive oil and season with salt and pepper. Sear on each side in a very hot skillet for 1 to 2 minutes. Refrigerate the tuna while preparing the vegetables. Combine the red cabbage, napa cabbage and carrots in a large bowl and mix well. Cut the tuna into cubes. Toss the tuna, avocado, red onion and scallions together in a bowl. Toss the cabbage mixture with a small amount of the Asian Vinaigrette in a salad bowl. Pour the remaining Asian Vinaigrette over the tuna mixture and toss to coat. Layer over the cabbage mixture.

Yield: 4 entrée servings

SRIRACHA

Sriracha is a Southeast Asian hot sauce from Thailand, named after the seaside town Si Racha, where it was first produced. It's made from sun-ripened chile peppers, vinegar, garlic, sugar, and salt.

Asian Vinaigrette

1/2 cup olive oil
2/3 cup lime juice
Zest of 1 lime
4 tablespoons soy sauce
2 tablespoons sesame oil
2 tablespoons wasabi powder
2 teaspoons sriracha (see sidebar)
2 teaspoons pickled ginger, chopped
1 tablespoon chopped fresh cilantro

Whisk the olive oil, lime juice, lime zest, soy sauce, sesame oil, wasabi powder, sriracha, pickled ginger and cilantro together in a small bowl. Adjust the spiciness as desired.

Yield: about 1 1/2 cups

Miso-Glazed Halibut

This recipe requires overnight refrigeration.
Substitute bass for halibut, if desired.

1 cup white (shiro) miso
1/4 cup sake
1/4 cup mirin or medium-dry sherry
1 tablespoon dark brown sugar
4 (6-ounce) halibut fillets
1 teaspoon extra-virgin olive oil

Combine the miso, sake, mirin and brown sugar in a small saucepan. Bring to a boil over medium heat. Reduce the heat to low and simmer for 2 minutes, stirring occasionally. Place in a small bowl and cool completely. Spread 1/3 of the miso marinade in a glass baking dish. Add the halibut fillets skin side down. Spread the remaining marinade over the fillets. Marinate, covered with plastic wrap, in the refrigerator for 12 to 24 hours. Scrape the marinade from the fillets and pat dry. Brush with the olive oil. Grill for 8 minutes or until the fish flakes easily, turning once.

Yield: 4 servings

Asparagus in Hazelnut Butter

1 pound asparagus spears, trimmed
2 tablespoons butter
2 tablespoons chopped hazelnuts
Salt and pepper to taste

Cook the asparagus in boiling water in a saucepan until tender-crisp; drain and remove to a serving dish. Melt the butter in a small skillet and stir in the hazelnuts. Sauté over low heat until the butter is golden brown; do not allow the butter to burn. Spoon over the asparagus.

Yield: 4 servings

TIP: Female asparagus stalks are more plump and tender than the thin male varieties.

CLARIFIED BUTTER FOR SAUTÉING

Use clarified butter in place of regular butter when sautéing or stir-frying. Clarified butter doesn't burn as easily and keeps in the refrigerator for two months.

To make clarified butter, melt the desired amount of butter in a saucepan over low heat. As water evaporates, the milk solids will form a white residue in the pan. As soon as these solids form, remove the pan from the heat; don't allow the solids to brown. Cool for fifteen minutes. Pour the clear butter into a storage jar and discard the white solids.

Roasted Spring Vegetables

1/2 cup extra-virgin olive oil
1 onion, sliced
1/2 teaspoon basil
1/4 teaspoon oregano
3 zucchini, sliced
3 yellow squash, sliced
1 red bell pepper, sliced
1 green bell pepper, sliced
10 ounces fresh green beans
1/4 cup extra-virgin olive oil
2 Roma tomatoes, quartered,
    or 1 (8-ounce) can whole tomatoes
2 tablespoons water
    (if fresh tomatoes are used)
Kosher salt and pepper to taste

Combine 1/2 cup olive oil, the onion, basil and oregano in a large glass baking dish and mix well. Bake in a preheated 350-degree oven for 5 to 8 minutes or until the onion is a light caramel color. Add the zucchini, yellow squash, bell peppers and green beans. Drizzle with 1/4 cup olive oil. Bake for 10 minutes or until the bell peppers are tender, stirring occasionally. Add the Roma tomatoes and water or add the canned tomatoes, quartered, along with their juice. Bake for 5 minutes longer. Add salt and pepper.

Yield: 8 to 10 servings.

TIP: To make a pasta primavera, omit the green beans in this recipe and serve the vegetables over pasta that has been tossed in olive oil, basil, salt, and pepper.

Mexican Rice

2 tablespoons butter
2¹/₂ tablespoons vegetable oil
1 yellow onion, chopped
2 tablespoons minced shallots
2 cups uncooked basmati rice
2¹/₂ teaspoons cumin
2 teaspoons oregano

3 cups chicken stock
1 (14-ounce) can diced tomatoes
8 ounces feta cheese, crumbled
 or cubed
1 cup chopped roasted red and
 yellow bell peppers

Heat the butter and oil in a skillet over medium heat. Add the onion and shallots and sauté for 5 minutes or until translucent. Stir in the rice, cumin and oregano. Cook for 3 minutes, stirring frequently. Add the chicken stock and tomatoes. Bring to a boil. Stir in the cheese and bell peppers. Simmer, covered, for 5 to 6 minutes or until the liquid is absorbed. Remove from the heat and let stand for 10 minutes. Fluff the rice with a fork.

Yield: 6 to 8 servings

TIP: For the best Mexican-style rice, rinse long grain white rice and sauté it in canola oil until brown before adding the liquid. Equal portions of chicken broth and tomatoes canned with their liquid are ideal for use as the liquid. Use a 2:1 ratio of liquid to rice. Stir in a little tomato paste to add flavor, color, and texture. Garlic and jalapeño chiles may also be added; sauté the desired amount and add to the mixture. For garnishes, top the rice with chopped fresh cilantro, minced jalapeños, and a squirt of fresh lime juice.

THE SPICE HOUSE ADDS SOME KICK

Spice up these dishes with one of The Spice House's specialty Chicago seasonings: Pilsen Latino Seasoning. Named for an area of Chicago with a strong Hispanic/Latino population, this blend has some real zest. It's ideal for salsa, beans, burritos, rice, and beef. Stop by The Spice House at Wells Street in Chicago or Evanston to find some.

Chocolate Fudge Brownie

This recipe was provided by the Executive Chef of
The Palmer House Hilton, Chicago.

BROWNIE	GLAZE
18 ounces semisweet chocolate	1 cup water
2 cups (4 sticks) butter	1 cup apricot preserves
1¹/₂ pounds sugar (about 3¹/₃ cups)	1 teaspoon unflavored gelatin
8 ounces cake flour (about 2¹/₃ cups)	
1 tablespoon baking powder	
4 eggs	
1 pound walnuts, crushed	

For the brownie, melt the chocolate with the butter in a double boiler over simmering water. Combine the sugar, flour and baking powder in a mixing bowl. Add the chocolate mixture and beat for 4 to 5 minutes. Beat in the eggs. Pour into a greased 9×12-inch baking pan. Sprinkle with the walnuts and press them lightly into the batter. Bake in a preheated 300-degree oven for 30 to 40 minutes or until the edges are crispy and the brownie is about ¹/₄ inch high. The center will still be moist. Let stand at room temperature for 30 minutes.

For the glaze, combine the water, preserves and gelatin in a small saucepan and mix well. Bring to a boil and simmer for 2 minutes. Pour the hot glaze over the brownies.

Yield: 12 to 15 servings

TIP: The brownies are easier to cut if you freeze them
for three to four hours after glazing.

The first reference to the "brownie" in America appears in the Sears Roebuck catalog published in Chicago in 1898. Specifically at the direction of Bertha Palmer to be served at the World's Columbian Exposition (also known as the Chicago World's Fair) in 1893, the brownie was created in the Palmer House kitchen. The recipe above is well over a century old and is the exact same one served in the Palmer House Hilton today. It remains one of the hotel's most popular confections.

Lemon Bars

SHORTBREAD CRUST
1/2 cup sifted confectioners' sugar
2 cups sifted all-purpose flour
1 cup (2 sticks) butter

LEMON FILLING
4 eggs, beaten
2 cups sugar
1/3 cup lemon juice
1/4 cup all-purpose flour
1/2 teaspoon baking powder
Confectioners' sugar

For the crust, combine the confectioners' sugar and flour in a bowl. Cut in the butter until crumbly. Press into a greased 9×13-inch baking pan. Bake in a preheated 350-degree oven for 20 to 25 minutes or until light brown.

For the filling, beat the eggs, sugar and lemon juice together in a small bowl. Combine the flour and baking powder and stir into the egg mixture. Pour over the baked crust. Bake in a preheated 350-degree oven for 25 minutes. Cool thoroughly and cut into 24 bars. Sprinkle with confectioners' sugar.

Yield: 24 servings

THE CHICAGO WORLD'S FAIR

The World's Columbian Exposition—also called the Chicago World's Fair—was held in 1893 to celebrate the four hundredth anniversary of Christopher Columbus's discovery of the New World. The exposition was located in Jackson Park and on the Midway Pleasance, a 630-acre piece of land in the neighborhoods of Hyde Park and Woodlawn. Frederick Law Olmsted laid out the fairgrounds, and Daniel Burnham was responsible for the architecture. Most of the buildings were based on classical architecture, and the area taken up by the fair around the Court of Honor was known as "The White City." The Ferris wheel made its debut at the fair, as did many foods that are now American favorites, including Aunt Jemina pancake mix, Cracker Jacks, Cream of Wheat, Quaker Oats, Juicy Fruit gum, Shredded Wheat, and the ice cream cone.

Oatmeal Caramel Cookie Bars

1 cup all-purpose flour
1 cup rolled oats
3/4 cup packed brown sugar
1/2 teaspoon baking soda
1/4 teaspoon salt
3/4 cup (1 1/2 sticks) butter, melted
32 caramels
1/2 cup evaporated milk
6 ounces semisweet chocolate chips
1/2 cup chopped nuts (optional)

Combine the flour, oats, brown sugar, baking soda, salt and melted butter in a bowl and mix well. Press into a greased 11×17-inch baking pan (this will make a very thin layer). Bake in a preheated 350-degree oven for 10 minutes. Combine the caramels and evaporated milk in a saucepan. Cook over low heat until melted and smooth, stirring constantly. Sprinkle the chocolate chips and nuts over the warm oatmeal crust and pour the warm caramel mixture evenly over the top. Bake for 15 to 20 minutes longer, being careful not to overbake. Cool for at least 20 minutes. Cut into squares.

Yield: 18 to 20 servings

Hummingbird Cake

CAKE
3 cups all-purpose flour
2 cups sugar
1 teaspoon baking soda
1 teaspoon cinnamon
1 teaspoon salt
3 eggs, beaten
$1^1/2$ cups vegetable oil
2 cups chopped bananas
1 (8-ounce) can juice-pack crushed pineapple
1 cup chopped nuts
$1^1/2$ teaspoons vanilla extract

CREAM CHEESE FROSTING
1 cup (2 sticks) butter, softened
16 ounces cream cheese, softened
1 (1-pound) package confectioners' sugar
2 teaspoons vanilla extract
1 cup chopped nuts

For the cake, combine the flour, sugar, baking soda, cinnamon and salt in a large mixing bowl. Add the eggs and oil and stir just until mixed. Stir in the bananas, pineapple, nuts and vanilla. Spoon into three greased 9-inch cake pans. Bake in a preheated 350-degree oven for 25 to 30 minutes. Cool in the pan for 10 minutes. Remove to a wire rack to cool completely.

For the frosting, cream the butter and cream cheese in a mixing bowl until light and fluffy. Beat in the confectioners' sugar and vanilla. Spread between the layers and over the top and side of the cake, sprinkling each layer with the nuts.

Yield: 8 to 10 servings

Rich Rum Bundt Cake

RUM CAKE
1 (2-layer) package butter or yellow cake mix
1 (3-ounce) package French vanilla
   instant pudding mix
$1/2$ cup water
$1/2$ cup white rum
$1/2$ cup vegetable oil
5 eggs
$1/2$ cup chopped pecans (optional)

RUM SAUCE
1 cup sugar
$1/4$ cup white rum
$1/4$ cup water

For the cake, combine the cake mix, pudding mix, water, rum, oil and eggs in a large bowl and mix well. Sprinkle the pecans over the bottom of a greased and floured bundt pan. Pour in the cake batter. Bake in a preheated 300-degree oven for 1 hour or until the cake tests done.

For the rum sauce, combine the sugar, rum and water in a saucepan. Bring to a boil over medium-high heat. Cook until of a syrupy consistency, stirring frequently.

Punch holes in the warm cake with a wooden skewer. Pour the rum sauce evenly over the cake. Cool in the pan for 45 minutes. Invert onto a serving plate.

Yield: 8 servings

Key Lime Cake

This cake is best served when prepared a day ahead.

1 (2-layer) package lemon cake mix
1 (6-ounce) package lemon instant
pudding mix
1 cup water
1 cup vegetable oil
4 eggs
2 teaspoons Key lime juice
9 cups confectioners' sugar
$^1/_2$ cup Key lime juice

Prepare and bake the cake mix using the package directions. Add the pudding mix, water, oil, eggs and 2 teaspoons lime juice one at a time and in the order listed, beating well after each addition. Pour into a greased and floured bundt pan. Bake in a preheated 325-degree oven for 50 to 60 minutes. Cool in the pan for 10 minutes. Combine the confectioners' sugar and $^1/_2$ cup lime juice in a bowl and mix well. Pierce the cake at intervals with a wooden skewer and pour the glaze over the top. Let stand for 2 hours. Invert onto a serving plate.

Yield: 8 servings

Mango and Lime Ice

2 mangoes, chopped
Zest and juice of 2 limes
$^1/_3$ cup sugar
$^1/_3$ cup water

Combine the mangoes; lime zest, lime juice, sugar and water in a blender and process until smooth. Pour into four glasses or dishes and freeze for 1 hour.

Yield: 4 servings

TIP: You may wish to make this dessert just before starting dinner. Consider serving smaller servings between courses rather than as dessert.

Chocolate Chip Cheesecake

24 Oreo cookies, crushed
2 tablespoons melted butter
24 ounces cream cheese, softened
1 (14-ounce) can sweetened condensed milk
3 eggs
1 teaspoon vanilla extract
6 ounces semisweet chocolate chips

Combine the cookie crumbs and butter in a bowl and mix well. Press into an ungreased springform pan. Combine the cream cheese, condensed milk, eggs and vanilla in a bowl and beat until smooth. Pour over the cookie crust. Sprinkle the chocolate chips evenly over the top. Bake in a preheated 350-degree oven for 1 hour. Remove to a wire rack to cool slightly. Chill in the refrigerator for 3 hours.

Yield: 8 to 10 servings

Grasshopper Pie

This recipe requires six to twelve hours of freezing.

1 cup chocolate wafer crumbs (about 20 cookies)
2 tablespoons butter, melted
1 (7-ounce) jar marshmallow creme
2 tablespoons milk
1/4 cup green crème de menthe
2 tablespoons white crème de cacao
8 ounces whipped topping
3 cups vanilla ice cream, softened
2 teaspoons chocolate syrup

Mix the cookie crumbs and butter in a small bowl. Press onto the bottom of a 9-inch springform pan. Chill the crust while making the filling. Combine the marshmallow creme and milk in a microwave-safe bowl. Microwave on High for 1 minute, stirring once. Stir in the crème de menthe, crème de cacao and whipped topping. Spread the vanilla ice cream over the cookie crust. Top with the marshmallow creme mixture. Freeze for 6 hours or longer. Drizzle with the chocolate syrup before serving.

Yield: 12 servings

SUMMER

Summer in Chicago is every city dweller's dream. It's the one time of year that begs for outdoor activity, and

Chicagoans take full advantage of the warmer weather in earnest. Whether it's a picnic or movie at

Millennium Park or Grant Park, a summer music or arts festival, the Chicago Symphony, baseball, or the lakefront,

our city calls us to celebrate the out-of-doors in that only-in-Chicago way.

And, what's summer without fresh produce? Many of the city neighborhoods are hosts to farmers markets,

where you can buy fruits and vegetables directly from the people who grow them.

The Green City Market, Movies in the Park, Mac Race, and other summer menus in PEELING THE WILD ONION

feature a variety of items.

SUMMER

SUMMER MENUS

MAC RACE

Breakfast Casserole, 55

Mexican Flank Steak, 69

Corn Salsa, 69

Espresso Chocolate Walnut Brownies, 85

Sour Cream Coffee Cake, 55

"The Mac," a prestigious Chicago Yacht Club tradition, celebrates its one hundredth anniversary in 2008. It is the world's longest annual freshwater sailboat race, starting in Chicago and ending 333 miles away on Mackinac Island.

Offering a variety of foods the crew will enjoy helps boost energy and morale and can address many concerns particular to eating at sea. Race boats generally don't have well-equipped kitchens due to weight concerns, and the crew sometimes has to eat under less-than-ideal weather conditions. Keeping food stored at safe temperatures using only ice or dry ice, reheating food, and proper packaging are among the many concerns. And the weather forecast is important; if high winds and cold weather are expected, a good choice might be to bring chili on board.

It is widely believed that having a banana on board is bad luck. This superstition is thought to have originated in the early 1700s, when nearly every ship that disappeared at sea was carrying bananas in its cargo.

MOVIES IN THE PARK

Rice Salad with Lemon, Dill and Red Onion, 63

Pepper Quesadillas, 60

Flank Steak and Portobello Mushroom Sandwich, 68

Baked Caramel Popcorn, 92

The Chicago Outdoor Film Festival takes place every Tuesday evening from mid-July through August. Admission is free. Movies begin at sunset in Grant Park, walking distance from the Chicago Loop. Now considered a Chicago tradition, this one-of-a-kind outdoor theater experience features a classic film on a gigantic screen (34×50 feet) and a state-of-the-art sound system. The festival also features a short film by a local filmmaker prior to the night's feature presentation. It is a great place to meet after work, and most viewers bring a picnic to enjoy on the grounds.

Ravinia Festival is the oldest outdoor music festival in North America and is lauded for presenting world-class music. The festival attracts about 600,000 listeners to 150 events representing a variety of genres. It was originally created as an amusement park in 1904 to service a nearby railroad. A group of North Shore residents purchased the park and reopened it in 1911. Ravinia became primarily a summer venue for classical music and was known as America's summer opera capital. In 1936, Ravinia became the summer residence of the Chicago Symphony Orchestra, which remains the centerpiece of the music festival today.

SUMMER MENUS

GREEN CITY MARKET

Peach Basil Iced Tea, 54

Veggie Ceviche, 64

Tomatoes and Goat Cheese Crostini, 57

Skewers of Rosemary Chicken and Zucchini, 66

Salmon Cakes with Lemon Caper Mayonnaise, 74

Mixed Berries with Berry Coulis, 91

The year 2006 marked the twenty-seventh anniversary of the Chicago Farmers Markets. Markets are held Tuesday, Wednesday, Thursday, Saturday, and Sunday in different neighborhoods around the city from May to October. Farmers and producers who grow or produce their own products apply to the city to participate. Featured items include organic and nonorganic fruits and vegetables, fresh herbs, breads, flowers, honey, jam, pies, nuts, and plants.

Over forty sustainable and certified organic farmers, all of whom own small family farms, participate in Chicago's Green City Market. The Green Market Café serves crepes, panini, burgers, and pastries, all with ingredients sourced from local farmers. The market has chef cooking demonstrations, education programs, discussions on health and nutrition, a membership base that provides funding, a volunteer group, an inviting ambience, a sense of community, and much more. Alice Waters has called the Green City Market "the best sustainable market in the country," and many popular local restaurants buy their fresh produce from the farmers who participate.

JAZZ FESTIVAL

Cold Cucumber Soup with Crab Meat, 66

Thyme-Scented Goat Cheese Cakes with
Balsamic Dijon Vinaigrette, 57

Zucchini Soufflé, 84

Herb-Baked Scallops, 80

Marvelous Mocha Pie, 88

The Chicago Jazz Festival started when several dozen Chicago musicians held a festival to honor Duke Ellington after his death in 1974. Ten thousand music lovers came, marking the first of what would become annual memorial concerts that drew crowds of up to 30,000. In 1978, musicians, working with Chicago's Council of Fine Arts, held the first John Coltrane Memorial Concert in Grant Park, another popular success. The following year the Jazz Institute of Chicago began planning its own festival in August. These three festivals were later rolled into one. Typically held Labor Day weekend, the Chicago Jazz Festival now consists of four days of free concerts held on three stages in Grant Park.

Jazz musicians came to Chicago as part of the Great Migration. Between 1916 and the end of the 1920s, some 75,000 Southern immigrants arrived on the South Side of Chicago. By the time Freddie Keppard, Sidney Bechet, Lee Collins, King Oliver, and other musicians arrived in 1918, the classic New Orleans style had already begun to change in deference to local tastes. Chicago expected hard-driving, up-tempo playing, and elegantly turned-out musicians in sophisticated surroundings. This scene inspired musicians from all over town; white musicians would appear in South Side clubs, among them Jimmy McPartland, Bud Freeman, Frank Teschemacher, Dave Tough, Gene Krupa, Muggsy Spanier, and Eddie Condon, who would collectively be credited with the creation of the Chicago jazz style of the twenties.

Peach Basil Iced Tea

3 orange pekoe tea bags
1 cup loosely packed fresh basil leaves
5 cups water
1/2 cup sugar
1 (15-ounce) can peach nectar, chilled
Peach slices (optional)
Sprigs of basil (optional)

Combine the tea bags and basil leaves in a large glass measure or heatproof bowl. Bring the water to a boil in a saucepan and pour over the tea bags. Steep for 5 minutes; strain through a sieve into a heatproof pitcher. Add the sugar and stir until dissolved. Cool and refrigerate, covered, for 1 hour or until cold. Stir in the peach nectar. Serve over ice in tall glasses. Garnish with peach slices and sprigs of basil.

Yield: about 7 cups

STIR UP A SANGRIA

Sangria is a perfect summer picnic beverage. It is a Spanish drink made of dry red wine, sliced fruit, Triple Sec or brandy, and sugar. Mix the sangria up several hours before you intend to drink it, so the flavors have time to blend. If white wine is used instead of red, it's called sangria blanca.

Whamboozie

4 (12-ounce) cans frozen lemonade
   concentrate, thawed
12 bottles beer (light beer works best)
1 (750-milliliter) bottle
   citrus-flavored vodka

Combine the lemonade concentrate, beer and vodka with ice in a punch bowl or other large container and mix well.

Yield: 1 gallon of fun

TIP: Reduce or increase this recipe according to the size of your crowd. Just remember the ratio of three cans of beer to each can of lemonade concentrate.

WARNING: This drink goes down easily but packs a punch.

Raspberry Orange Sunrises

4 cups fresh orange juice
   (about 8 oranges)
1 cup frozen unsweetened raspberries
1 1/2 cups semisweet sparkling wine
3 orange slices, halved (optional)

Combine the orange juice and raspberries in a blender and process until smooth. Pour into a pitcher and stir in the wine. Pour over ice and garnish each glass with an orange slice.

Yield: 6 servings

Breakfast Casserole

1 pound bulk pork sausage (mild or spicy)
10 eggs
2 cups milk
$^1/_2$ cup chopped fresh chives
2 teaspoons dry mustard
1 teaspoon kosher salt
1 teaspoon pepper
8 slices white bread, cut into cubes
8 to 12 ounces goat cheese, crumbled
$^1/_4$ cup chopped parsley (optional)
1 tomato, sliced (optional)

Brown the sausage in a skillet, stirring until crumbly; drain. Whisk the eggs, milk, chives, dry mustard, salt and pepper together in a bowl. Arrange the bread cubes in a 9×13-inch baking dish coated with nonstick cooking spray. Layer the sausage and cheese over the bread. Pour the egg mixture over the top. (The casserole can be baked at this point or refrigerated for several hours. Bring to room temperature before baking.) Bake in a preheated 350-degree oven for 50 minutes or until a knife inserted in the center comes out clean. Garnish with parsley and tomato slices. Cool slightly before serving.

Yield: 8 servings

TIP: For added richness, butter the bread slices before cutting them into cubes. If you want to add other vegetables, such as mushrooms, be sure to sauté them to remove excess moisture before adding them to the casserole. Add a weight to the covered strata while it is chilling overnight; this will improve the texture. Use of a spicy sausage will add a little kick to the casserole.

Sour Cream Coffee Cake

1 cup (2 sticks) unsalted butter, softened
2 cups granulated sugar
2 eggs, beaten
2 cups sour cream
1 tablespoon vanilla extract
2 cups all-purpose flour
1 tablespoon baking powder
$^1/_4$ teaspoon salt
1$^1/_2$ cups pecans, chopped
$^3/_4$ cup packed brown sugar
1 tablespoon cinnamon

Cream the butter and granulated sugar in a bowl until light and fluffy. Add the eggs, sour cream and vanilla, beating well after each addition. Sift the flour, baking powder and salt together in a bowl. Add to the creamed mixture and stir just until mixed. Combine the pecans, brown sugar and cinnamon in a bowl and mix well. Pour half the batter into a greased and floured bundt pan. Top with half the pecan mixture. Repeat the layers. Bake in a preheated 350-degree oven for 1 hour or until the cake tests done. Cool in the pan for 10 minutes. Invert onto a serving plate.

Yield: 8 servings

Bread Pudding Pancakes with Vanilla Custard Sauce and Cinnamon-Sugar Butter

This recipe was provided by the Executive Chefs of Southport Grocery.

CINNAMON-SUGAR BUTTER
1 cup (2 sticks) unsalted butter
1/4 teaspoon salt
2 teaspoons ground cinnamon
2 tablespoons sugar

VANILLA CUSTARD SAUCE
2 cups heavy cream
1 vanilla bean
6 tablespoons sugar
4 egg yolks, beaten

PANCAKES
14 slices firm white bread
2 1/2 cups milk
1 1/4 cups all-purpose flour
3 tablespoons sugar
1 tablespoon baking powder
1 teaspoon salt
2 eggs, beaten
1 teaspoon vegetable oil
2 tablespoons butter

For the cinnamon-sugar butter, melt 1/2 cup of the butter in a small saucepan. Add the salt, cinnamon and sugar and cook until the sugar is dissolved, stirring constantly. Add the remaining 1/2 cup butter and whisk with a hand mixer until creamy and fluffy.

For the sauce, place the cream in a saucepan. Cut the vanilla bean into halves lengthwise. Scrape the seeds into the cream and add the vanilla bean pod. Bring to a simmer. Whisk the sugar and egg yolks in a bowl until smooth. Whisk 1/4 cup of the hot cream mixture into the egg yolk mixture to temper. Whisk the egg yolk mixture into the hot cream. Simmer until the sauce is thickened and coats the back of a wooden spoon, stirring constantly. Remove from the heat and strain into a bowl, discarding the solids. Chill over an ice bath.

For the pancakes, trim the crusts from the bread. Cut the bread into 1-inch squares and place in a large bowl. Add the milk and let soak for 5 minutes or until softened. Mix the flour, sugar, baking powder and salt in a small bowl. Fold into the bread mixture until just about half incorporated. Add the eggs and oil and mix gently. Melt the butter in a skillet. Drop the batter by 1/3 cupfuls into the hot skillet and cook for 3 to 4 minutes on each side. The pancakes will have a moist bread pudding-like consistency inside. Serve topped with the cinnamon-sugar butter and a ramekin of the vanilla custard sauce on the side.

Yield: 6 servings

Thyme-Scented Goat Cheese Cakes with Balsamic Dijon Vinaigrette

GOAT CHEESE CAKES
1 (8-ounce) log goat cheese, cut into 12 rounds
3 tablespoons extra-virgin olive oil
1 tablespoon fresh thyme, chopped
1/4 cup bread crumbs
1 teaspoon dried thyme
1/4 teaspoon kosher salt
1/4 teaspoon crushed black peppercorns

BALSAMIC VINAIGRETTE
1/3 cup balsamic vinegar
1 teaspoon Dijon mustard
3/4 cup extra-virgin olive oil
Kosher salt and freshly ground pepper to taste

For the goat cheese cakes, place the goat cheese rounds in a shallow glass dish. Top with the olive oil and fresh thyme. Chill, covered, for 1 hour. Combine the bread crumbs, dried thyme, salt and pepper in a small bowl and mix well. Press into both sides of the goat cheese rounds. Bake on a baking sheet in a preheated 350-degree oven for 15 to 20 minutes or until golden brown.

For the vinaigrette, whisk the balsamic vinegar and mustard together in a small bowl. Add the olive oil in a steady stream, whisking constantly until thickened. Add salt and pepper.

Serve over the goat cheese cakes.

Yield: 6 appetizer servings

TIP: For either an entrée or appetizer salad, serve the goat cheese cakes over a bed of fresh greens.

Tomatoes and Goat Cheese Crostini

2 tablespoons finely chopped fresh basil
2 tablespoons finely chopped fresh parsley
2 tablespoons water
2 tablespoons fresh lemon juice
1 teaspoon extra-virgin olive oil
8 (1/4-inch-thick) slices baguette, cut on the diagonal
4 teaspoons goat cheese
20 (1/4-inch-thick) slices tomato
1/2 teaspoon kosher salt
1/2 teaspoon freshly ground pepper

Combine the basil, parsley, water, lemon juice and olive oil in a blender and process until smooth. Bake the baguette slices in a single layer on a baking sheet in a preheated 350-degree oven for 7 minutes or until crisp. Spread 1/2 teaspoon goat cheese over each slice. Divide the tomato slices among four salad plates. Drizzle 1 tablespoon of the herb mixture over each serving. Sprinkle each with 1/8 teaspoon salt and 1/8 teaspoon pepper. Add 2 crostini to each plate.

Yield: 4 servings

Vegetable Summer Rolls with Spicy Peanut Sauce

1 ounce cellophane noodles
1 tablespoon seasoned rice vinegar
Salt to taste
4 (8-inch) rice paper rounds (or more in case some tear)
4 Bibb lettuce leaves, ribs removed
Spicy Peanut Sauce (page 59)
1/4 cup chopped fresh basil leaves (preferably Thai basil)
1/2 cup thinly sliced red and yellow bell peppers
1/4 cup fresh cilantro leaves
1/2 cup arugula or other lettuce
1/3 cup coarsely shredded carrot (1 medium)

Soak the cellophane noodles in boiling water to cover for 15 minutes; drain and pat dry between paper towels. Combine the noodles, vinegar and salt in a small bowl and mix well. Soak 1 rice paper round in warm water in a shallow baking dish for 30 to 60 seconds. Discard the round if it has any holes and begin with a new round. Drain on a double thickness of paper towels.

Arrange 1 Bibb lettuce leaf on the bottom half of the soaked rice pepper, folding or tearing the lettuce to fit and leaving a 1-inch border. Spread 1 tablespoon Spicy Peanut Sauce over the lettuce. Top with 1/4 each of the noodles, basil, bell peppers, cilantro, arugula and carrot. Roll up the rice paper tightly around the filling, tucking in the ends. Repeat with the remaining rice paper rounds and filling. Remove the rolls to a serving plate and cover with dampened paper towels. Cut the rolls in half on the diagonal. Serve with additional Spicy Peanut Sauce.

Yield: 4 servings

TIP: These rolls must be made one at a time to keep the wrappers moist.
Soak the rice paper rounds just long enough to be pliable. For added flavor,
marinate all the filling ingredients as well as the noodles.

Spicy Peanut Sauce

1 large garlic clove, crushed or minced
3/4 teaspoon hot red pepper flakes
1 teaspoon toasted sesame oil
3 tablespoons water
2 tablespoons seasoned rice wine vinegar
2 tablespoons creamy peanut butter
1 tablespoon hoisin sauce
1 tablespoon honey
1 tablespoon soy sauce
2 teaspoons tomato paste

Sauté the garlic and hot red pepper flakes in the sesame oil in a skillet for 3 minutes or until very pale gold, stirring constantly. Whisk in the water, rice wine vinegar, peanut butter, hoisin sauce, honey, soy sauce and tomato paste. Cook for 1 minute, whisking constantly. Cool completely.

Yield: about 2/3 cup

Crab Quesadillas

1/4 cup chopped green onions
1 jalapeño chile, seeded and finely chopped
1 tablespoon minced fresh cilantro
2 tablespoons sour cream
3/4 teaspoon minced garlic
1/2 cup (2 ounces) shredded Monterey Jack cheese
4 (8-inch) flour tortillas
8 ounces lump crab meat,
shells removed and flaked
Lime wedges

Mix the green onions, jalapeño chile, cilantro, sour cream and garlic in a bowl. Sprinkle 2 tablespoons of the cheese over each tortilla. Divide the crab meat evenly over the cheese. Fold the tortillas in half, pressing gently to seal. Broil on a baking sheet for 1 minute on each side or until lightly browned. (Or brown the quesadillas in a skillet coated with nonstick cooking spray.) Serve with the sour cream mixture, salsa and lime wedges.

Yield: 8 appetizer servings

Pepper Quesadillas

2 cups (8 ounces) shredded Monterey Jack cheese
4 (8-inch) flour tortillas
1 red or yellow bell pepper, cut into thin strips
1 jalapeño chile, thinly sliced
4 ounces soft goat cheese, crumbled
1 lime, cut into wedges

Sprinkle 1/2 cup Monterey Jack cheese over half of each tortilla. Top with 5 or 6 strips of bell pepper and slices of the jalapeño chile. Top each tortilla with 1 ounce goat cheese and a few drops of lime juice. Fold the tortillas in half and press lightly to seal. Brown 1 quesadilla at a time on both sides in a skillet over medium heat until the cheese is melted. Repeat with the remaining quesadillas. Serve with lime wedges.

Yield: 4 servings

Mediterranean Layered Salad

This recipe needs overnight refrigeration.

3/4 cup fresh lemon juice
(about 4 large lemons)
2 tablespoons extra-virgin olive oil
3 garlic cloves, minced
1 teaspoon salt
1 cup uncooked medium bulgur
2 cups finely chopped red onions
5 cups chopped tomatoes
(about 5 large tomatoes)
1/2 cup chopped fresh parsley
1/2 cup chopped fresh mint
1/4 cup chopped fresh dill weed
2 cups chopped seeded peeled cucumbers
1 cup chopped red bell pepper
3/4 teaspoon salt
1/4 teaspoon freshly ground pepper

Combine the lemon juice, olive oil, garlic and 1 teaspoon salt in a small bowl and mix well. Drizzle over the bulgur in a large serving bowl. Layer the onions, tomatoes, parsley, mint, dill weed, cucumbers and bell pepper over the bulgur mixture. Sprinkle with 3/4 teaspoon salt and the pepper. Chill, covered with plastic wrap, for 24 to 48 hours before serving.

Yield: 8 to 10 servings

TIP: This dish looks great layered in a glass trifle bowl.

Little Italy Panzanella

4 (1-ounce) slices Italian bread, crusts trimmed, cut into 1-inch cubes
2 pounds tomatoes, cored and cut into 1-inch pieces
1 (16-ounce) can cannellini or other white beans, rinsed and drained
1/2 cup thinly sliced red onion
1/3 cup pitted kalamata olives, halved
1 cup torn fresh basil leaves
3 tablespoons red wine vinegar
1 tablespoon water
1 tablespoon extra-virgin olive oil
1 teaspoon minced garlic
1/2 teaspoon freshly ground pepper
1/4 teaspoon salt

Arrange the bread cubes in a single layer on a baking sheet and coat with nonstick cooking spray. Bake in a preheated 350-degree oven for 15 minutes or until toasted. Combine the tomatoes, cannellini, onion, olives and basil in a serving bowl. Stir in the toasted bread cubes. Whisk the red wine vinegar, water, olive oil, garlic, pepper and salt together in a small bowl. Drizzle over the salad and toss well. Serve immediately.

Yield: 4 servings

Tomato and Black Olive Salad

8 tomatoes, each cut into 8 wedges
1 red onion, sliced
2 cups black olives
1 cup chopped fresh basil
1/4 cup extra-virgin olive oil
2 tablespoons balsamic vinegar
1 1/4 tablespoons grainy mustard
Fresh rosemary to taste
Salt and pepper to taste

Toss the tomato wedges, onion, olives and basil together in a salad bowl. Whisk the olive oil, balsamic vinegar, mustard and rosemary together in a small bowl. Pour over the tomato mixture and toss gently. Season with salt and pepper.

Yield: 4 to 6 servings

HAMBURGER GRILLING TIPS

Use 80 percent lean chuck for a juicier burger.

Add a panade to the patty. Panade is a paste made from bread and milk and is often used to keep meat loaf and meatballs moist.

Add minced garlic and a tangy steak sauce to the patty for added flavor.

If you make a slight depression in the center of the patty before grilling, it will puff slightly as it cooks and result in a burger with a level top.

Grilled Chicken Salad with Grapes and Cashews

4 large boneless, skinless chicken breasts
Olive oil
Salt and freshly ground pepper to taste
1 cup grapes, halved
3/4 cup mayonnaise
1/2 cup chopped green onions
1/4 cup chopped red onion
1/4 cup cashews, chopped and toasted
1/4 cup chopped fresh parsley

Rub each chicken breast with a little olive oil and season with salt and pepper. Grill until cooked through. Let stand until cool. Chill in the refrigerator until cold. Combine the grapes, mayonnaise, green onions, red onion, cashews and parsley in a large bowl and mix well. Cut the chicken into bite-size cubes. Add to the grape mixture and mix well. Season with salt and pepper.

Yield: 4 to 6 servings

Shrimp and Scallop Salad

2 pounds peeled cooked shrimp
2 pounds cooked scallops
2 cups diced celery
2 cups sliced water chestnuts
2 cups mayonnaise
1 (16-ounce) can pineapple
chunks, drained
1/2 cup minced green onions
2 tablespoons soy sauce
4 tablespoons lemon juice
1 tablespoon curry powder
2 cups toasted almonds

Combine the shrimp, scallops, celery, water chestnuts, mayonnaise, pineapple chunks, green onions, soy sauce, lemon juice and curry powder in a large bowl and mix well. Chill thoroughly. Top with the almonds.

Yield: 12 servings

ADD A LITTLE DILL

Traditionally, dill weed is heavily used in German and Scandinavian cooking. Dill weed's flavor—lighter and sweeter than dill seed— along with its bright green, feathery leaves, makes it a perfect addition to omelets, cheese sauces, salad dressings, and dips. Dill is traditionally added to any dish with a white sauce, from potato salad to sour cream dips. It is nice as a garnish, or sprinkled on salad, soup, or chicken.

Rice Salad with Lemon, Dill and Red Onion

3/4 teaspoon coarse salt
1 cup uncooked long grain white rice
1/3 cup finely chopped red onion
3 tablespoons red wine vinegar
Juice of 1 lemon
21/2 tablespoons extra-virgin olive oil
2 teaspoons finely chopped garlic
1/2 teaspoon freshly ground pepper
3 tablespoons coarsely chopped
fresh dill weed
Zest of 1 lemon

Fill a medium saucepan three-quarters full with water and bring to a boil. Add the salt and rice. Bring back to a boil. Reduce the heat and simmer for 15 minutes. Drain through a sieve. Remove to a serving bowl. Combine the red onion and vinegar in a small bowl. Let stand for 5 minutes. Strain through a sieve, discarding the vinegar. Whisk the lemon juice, olive oil, garlic and pepper together in a small bowl. Pour over the rice. Add the onion, dill weed and lemon zest and toss gently.

Yield: 4 servings

TIP: Try substituting orzo for the rice in this dish.

Greek Tuna Salad

1 (6-ounce) can tuna in olive oil,
lightly drained
1 (6-ounce) jar artichoke hearts,
drained and halved lengthwise
8 ounces cherry tomatoes
1/2 English cucumber, halved lengthwise
and cut into 1/4-inch slices
6 ounces feta cheese, cut into 1/4-inch cubes
1/3 cup pitted kalamata olives
1 tablespoon mayonnaise
1 tablespoon balsamic vinegar

Combine the tuna, artichoke hearts, cherry tomatoes, cucumber, cheese, olives, mayonnaise and balsamic vinegar in a bowl and mix well.

Yield: 6 servings

Veggie Ceviche

1 large tomato, diced
1 (14-ounce) can artichoke hearts,
drained and quartered
4 ounces sliced fresh mushrooms
1/4 cup chopped green onions
3 tablespoons extra-virgin olive oil
1 garlic clove, minced
1/4 cup lime juice
1 avocado, sliced into bite-size pieces
Pita chips

Combine the tomato, artichoke hearts, mushrooms, green onions, olive oil, garlic and lime juice in a bowl. Chill for at least 15 minutes. Stir in the avocado just before serving.

Serve with pita chips.

Yield: 8 to 12 servings

TIP: Ceviche is traditionally a dish of very fresh seafood marinated, or "cooked," in citrus juice and served as a first course or main course salad. This recipe is a veggie-only version of this Latin dish.
This is a refreshing appetizer for summer barbecues.

Broccoli Salad with Bacon and Red Onion

Make this salad three to four hours ahead of time and chill it until serving time.

Florets of 1 large bunch broccoli
1/2 cup chopped red onion
1 cup (4 ounces) shredded sharp
Cheddar cheese
1 cup mayonnaise
1/2 cup sugar
1 tablespoon vinegar
8 to 10 slices bacon, crisp-cooked
and crumbled

Combine the broccoli florets, onion and cheese in a salad bowl. Whisk the mayonnaise, sugar and vinegar together in a small bowl. Pour over the broccoli mixture and toss to combine. Top with the crumbled bacon.

Yield: 8 to 10 servings

TIP: You may enjoy an addition of sunflower seeds, chopped walnuts, chopped pecans, or other favorite nut.

Corn Chowder

1 onion, chopped
2 large garlic cloves, minced
1/4 cup (1/2 stick) butter
1 cup minced bell pepper
1 stalk celery, minced
1 1/2 cups corn kernels
2 (14-ounce) cans cream-style corn
2 cups whipping cream
2 fresh cayenne chiles, minced
1 tablespoon honey
1/2 teaspoon white pepper
Salt and pepper to taste
1 pound shrimp, peeled and deveined

Sauté the onion and garlic in the butter in a skillet for 1 minute. Add the bell pepper and celery. Cook for 1 minute. Stir in the corn kernels, cream-style corn, whipping cream, cayenne chiles, honey and white pepper. Simmer for 15 minutes, stirring occasionally. Season with salt and pepper. Add the shrimp and simmer for 5 minutes. If shrimp are frozen, simmer for 15 minutes.

Yield: 6 servings

TIP: Use fresh sweet corn in this chowder when it's available.

Cold Cucumber Soup with Crab Meat

2 cucumbers, peeled, seeded and chopped
(about 3 cups)
2 cups (1-inch cubes) honeydew melon
2 yellow bell peppers, chopped (about 1 cup)
1 1/2 tablespoons finely chopped shallot (1 large)
1 jalapeño chile, seeded and chopped
1/2 cup plain yogurt
3 tablespoons fresh lime juice
Salt and pepper to taste
8 ounces lump crab meat,
shells removed and flaked
1 tablespoon extra-virgin olive oil
2 teaspoons white wine vinegar
3 tablespoons finely chopped fresh chives (optional)
Diced yellow bell pepper (optional)

Combine the cucumbers, honeydew melon, bell peppers, shallot, jalapeño chile, yogurt, lime juice, salt and pepper in a blender and process until smooth. Pass through a fine sieve into a bowl. Chill, covered, for 4 hours or until very cold. (Prepare up to a day ahead if desired.) Toss the crab meat, olive oil and white wine vinegar together in a small bowl. Season with salt and pepper. Divide the crab meat among six soup bowls, mounding it in the center. Ladle the soup around the crab meat. Garnish with the chives and diced yellow pepper.

Yield: 6 servings

Chicken Satay

3 pounds boneless skinless chicken breasts
1 cup coconut milk
2 tablespoons fish sauce
2 tablespoons fresh cilantro, chopped
4 teaspoons red curry paste
2 teaspoons brown sugar
1 teaspoon turmeric
Salt and pepper to taste
Spicy Peanut Sauce (page 59)

Cut each chicken breast lengthwise into three pieces. Combine the coconut milk, fish sauce, cilantro, red curry paste, brown sugar, turmeric, salt and pepper in a sealable plastic bag. Add the chicken and marinate in the refrigerator for several hours. Grill or roast the chicken in a preheated 400-degree oven for 20 minutes. Thread the chicken onto skewers and serve with Spicy Peanut Dipping Sauce.

Yield: 8 to 12 servings

Skewers of Rosemary Chicken and Zucchini

2 tablespoons grated lemon zest
1 tablespoon extra-virgin olive oil
1 1/2 tablespoons chopped fresh rosemary
1 teaspoon minced garlic
1 1/2 pounds boneless skinless
chicken breasts, cut into 3/4-inch pieces
2 tablespoons fresh lemon juice
1 tablespoon extra-virgin olive oil
1 teaspoon minced garlic
3/4 teaspoon salt
1/2 teaspoon pepper
1 1/4 pounds zucchini, cut into 3/4-inch pieces
Hot cooked rice

Combine the lemon zest, 1 tablespoon olive oil, the rosemary and 1 teaspoon garlic in a sealable plastic bag. Add the chicken and marinate in the refrigerator for at least 1 hour or overnight. Whisk the lemon juice, 1 tablespoon olive oil, 1 teaspoon garlic, the salt and pepper together in a small bowl. Thread the chicken and zucchini alternately onto twelve wooden skewers. Grill for 12 minutes or until the chicken is cooked through and the zucchini is tender, turning the skewers once. Drizzle with the lime juice mixture. Serve over rice.

Yield: 6 servings

TIP: To prevent the wooden skewers from burning on the grill, soak them
in water for several hours before threading the vegetables.

Flank Steak and Portobello Mushroom Sandwich

1 1/2 pounds flank steak,
scored across the grain
Extra-virgin olive oil
Salt and pepper to taste
4 portobello mushroom caps, sliced
1 Vidalia onion, cut into rings
1/4 cup balsamic vinegar

1/2 cup mayonnaise
1 tablespoon grated horseradish
Juice of 1/2 lemon
4 ciabatta bread loaves, split
1/4 pound sliced fontina cheese
1/2 cup arugula

Brush the flank steak with olive oil and season with salt and pepper. Broil 4 inches from the heat source for 4 to 5 minutes on each side. Arrange the mushrooms and onion in a single layer on a foil-lined baking sheet. Drizzle with the balsamic vinegar and a little olive oil and toss to coat. Broil for 8 to 10 minutes. Combine the mayonnaise, horseradish and lemon juice in a small bowl and mix well. Spread over both sides of the bread loaves. Slice the steak across the grain. Place several slices on the bottom halves of the bread loaves. Layer a mound of mushrooms and onion, slices of fontina cheese and arugula over the steak. Top with the remaining bread halves.

Yield: 4 servings

PORTOBELLOS

Both portobello mushrooms and
regular button mushrooms are from the
same strain of fungus; portobellos
are just left to grow larger. Because of their
large size and meaty texture, portobellos
are often grilled and used as a vegan or
lower-calorie substitute for burgers.

Mexican Flank Steak

4 tablespoons olive oil
3 tablespoons whole-grain mustard
2 tablespoons minced garlic
2 tablespoons dried Mexican oregano
2 tablespoons hot paprika
2 tablespoons cumin
Salt and pepper to taste
2 pounds flank steak

Mix the olive oil, whole-grain mustard, garlic, oregano, hot paprika, cumin, salt and pepper in a small bowl. Spread on both sides of the flank steak. Grill over hot coals for 7 minutes on each side for medium-rare or to desired degree of doneness. Let stand for a few minutes before slicing. Slice against the grain.

Serve with lime wedges and Corn Salsa (at right).

Yield: 4 to 6 servings

CORN ON THE COB

Boil corn in sugar-seasoned water to bring out the natural sweetness of the corn. Boiling corn in salted water produces a cob with tougher kernels. You may boil the corn in or out of its husk; corn cooked in its husk will pick up the husk's smell.

Corn Salsa

2 packages frozen corn
1 red bell pepper, diced
1 green bell pepper, diced
1 small red onion, diced
Jalapeño chiles, diced (optional)
1/3 cup olive oil
3 tablespoons maple syrup
1/2 cup chopped fresh parsley

Combine the corn, bell peppers, onion, jalapeño chiles, olive oil, maple syrup and parsley in a bowl and mix well.

Yield: 10 to 12 servings

Grilled Flank Steak

10$^{1}/_{2}$ tablespoons packed brown sugar
$^{1}/_{2}$ cup soy sauce
$^{1}/_{4}$ cup Worcestershire sauce
3 tablespoons vegetable oil

3 tablespoons red wine vinegar
1 teaspoon minced garlic
2 pounds flank steak

Combine the brown sugar, soy sauce, Worcestershire sauce, oil, red wine vinegar and garlic in a bowl and mix well. Prick holes with a meat fork in both sides of the flank steak. Pour the brown sugar mixture over the steak in a shallow dish. Marinate, covered, in the refrigeror for at least 4 hours and up to 24 hours, turning occasionally. Grill over hot coals to desired degree of doneness.

Yield: 4 to 6 servings

TIP: Flank steak has a rich, full, beefy flavor. It is thin, cooks quickly, and is thus ideal for grilling. Be sure to let the steak rest after grilling; this allows the juices to redistribute evenly throughout the meat before slicing.

TASTE OF CHICAGO 2006 FUN FOOD FACTS

CHOCOLATE-COVERED BANANAS: 45,000

BARBECUE CHICKEN: 5,200 pounds

BEEF ON A STICK: 9,000 servings

BREADED STEAK SANDWICHES: 45,000

BROWNIES: 5,500

CAJUN ALLIGATOR: 8,000 pounds

CARAMEL APPLES: 10,000

CATFISH: 19,000 pounds

CHEESEBURGERS: 52,000

CHEESECAKE: 118,000 slices

CHERRIES: 90,000 pounds

CHICKEN TENDERS: 10,000 servings

CHILI: 2,700 pounds

CHOCOLATE-COVERED STRAWBERRIES: 28,000 dipped in 2,200 pounds of chocolate

CHOCOLATE TURTLES: 35,000

CHOPPED CHICKEN LIME SALAD: 24,000 servings

CORN: 130,000 ears

CRAB LEGS: 25,000

CRAWFISH: 35,000 servings

Southwest Steak Wrap

1¹/₂ pounds skirt steak, diced
1¹/₂ tablespoons olive oil
¹/₄ cup tomato sauce
1¹/₂ tablespoons taco seasoning mix
Salt, black pepper and cayenne pepper to taste
4 (12-inch) sun-dried tomato wraps

4 pieces green leaf lettuce
1¹/₂ cups (6 ounces) shredded Monterey Jack cheese
¹/₃ cup canned black beans
¹/₃ cup frozen corn kernels, thawed
8 ounces guacamole

Sauté the skirt steak in the olive oil in a skillet for 1 minute. Stir in the tomato sauce, taco seasoning mix, salt, black pepper and cayenne pepper. Cook for a few minutes. Remove from the heat. Warm the wraps in a warm oven. Place a lettuce leaf on each wrap just below the center. Layer ¹/₄ of the steak, cheese, black beans, corn and guacamole over each lettuce leaf. Fold each side of the wrap toward the center. Roll up the wrap to form a tight cylinder. Repeat the process with the remaining wraps. Slice each wrap in half to serve.

Yield: 4 servings

MORE TASTE OF CHICAGO 2006 FUN FOOD FACTS

EGG ROLLS: 20,000

FRIED DOUGH: 20,000 servings

FRONTIER CHICKEN: 26,000 servings

ICE CREAM: 180,000 servings

ITALIAN FRIES: 5 tons

ITALIAN ICE: 10 tons

JERK CHICKEN: 24,000 pounds

MINI CANNOLIS: 14,000

PAD THAI: 25,000 servings

PIEROGI: 70,000

PIZZA: 175,000 slices

PLANTAIN CHIPS: 27,000 servings

POLISH SAUSAGE: 3,000 pounds

RIBS: 101,000 pounds

RIB SANDWICHES: 30,000

SAGANAKI (FRIED CHEESE): 150,000 servings

SAMOSAS (FRIED PIES): 12,000 pieces

SHRIMP: 32,600 servings

TACOS: 50,000

TOASTED RAVIOLI: 144,320

TURKEY LEGS: 45,000

Lemon Veal

2 pounds veal scallops
or boneless skinless chicken breasts
1/2 cup all-purpose flour
2 teaspoons salt
1/2 teaspoon freshly ground black pepper
Dash of cayenne pepper (optional)
4 tablespoons butter
4 tablespoons vegetable oil
or olive oil

4 tablespoons butter
1 tablespoon fresh tarragon,
or 1/4 teaspoon dried tarragon
(optional)
5 tablespoons fresh lemon juice
5 tablespoons chopped fresh parsley
4 cups cooked brown rice
1 lemon, thinly sliced (optional)
Additional parsley (optional)

Pound the veal 1/4 inch thick between sheets of waxed paper. Combine the flour, salt, black pepper and cayenne pepper in a sealable plastic bag. Add the veal and shake to coat evenly. Brown the veal on both sides in 4 tablespoons butter and the oil in a skillet. Place the veal on a dish and keep warm. Drain off the drippings. Add 4 tablespoons butter, the tarragon, lemon juice and 5 tablespoons parsley. Bring to a boil, stirring constantly. Add the veal and reheat in the sauce. Serve over the brown rice. Garnish with lemon slices and additional parsley.

Yield: 6 servings

VITELLO TONNATO

Leftover cooked veal can be turned into a simple version of this Italian classic. Slice the veal thinly, arrange on a serving platter, and chill. Combine 3 ounces drained canned tuna, 1 cup mayonnaise, 3 anchovy fillets, and 3 tablespoons heavy cream in a food processor and process until smooth. Thin as necessary with white wine. Season with cayenne pepper and lemon juice. Spoon over the chilled veal slices. Top with the flavored mayonnaise and sprinkle with capers.

Baja Halibut with Cumin Tartar Sauce

This recipe was provided by the Executive Chef of the Shedd Aquarium.

TARTAR SAUCE
3 cups mayonnaise
1/2 cup chopped dill pickles
1 tablespoon Dijon mustard
1 tablespoon Worcestershire sauce
1 tablespoon cumin
1 teaspoon sugar
Juice of 1/2 lemon (about 2 tablespoons)
Juice of 1/2 lime (about 2 teaspoons)

HALIBUT
3 pounds Alaskan halibut,
cut into 8 pieces
2 tablespoons cumin
Salt and pepper to taste
2 small limes, thinly sliced
1 red onion, julienned
1 avocado, sliced
1/2 cup chopped fresh cilantro

For the tartar sauce, whisk all the ingredients together in a bowl.

For the halibut, season the fish on both sides with the cumin, salt and pepper. Sear on a grill or in a sauté pan for 2 to 3 minutes on each side. Remove to a baking dish. Bake in a preheated 350-degree oven for 5 to 8 minutes or until the fish flakes easily. Top each serving with the lime slices, red onion, avocado and cilantro.

Serve with the Cumin Tartar Sauce.

Yield: 8 servings

Salmon Cakes with Lemon Caper Mayonnaise

1/4 cup finely chopped onion
1/4 cup finely chopped celery
1 teaspoon olive oil
2 (7-ounce) cans salmon, drained, flaked and boned
1 egg, lightly beaten
3/4 cup crushed saltines (about 20 crackers)
1 tablespoon Dijon mustard
1/4 teaspoon freshly ground pepper
2 teaspoons olive oil
Lemon Caper Mayonnaise (at right)

Sauté the onion and celery in 1 teaspoon olive oil in a skillet over medium heat for 4 minutes or until tender. Remove to a medium bowl. Add the salmon, egg, 1/2 cup of the crushed saltines, the mustard and pepper and mix well. Shape into four patties 1/2 inch thick. Coat with the remaining crushed saltines. Chill, covered, for 20 minutes. Heat 2 teaspoons olive oil in a large nonstick skillet over medium heat. Sauté the patties for 5 minutes on each side or until lightly browned. Serve with Lemon Caper Mayonnaise.

Yield: 4 servings

MAKE YOUR OWN MAYONNAISE

For 2 cups mayonnaise, process 1 egg and 2 egg yolks in a food processor for 30 seconds or until slightly thick. Add 1 teaspoon lemon juice or vinegar, 1/4 teaspoon dry mustard and salt to taste. With the machine running, add 1 cup vegetable oil very slowly. The mixture should be very thick. Add another cup of oil very slowly, processing the whole time. If the mayonnaise is too thick, thin with a few drops of lemon juice or vinegar. Season with salt, pepper and additional lemon juice or vinegar.

SAUCE TARTARE: Use hard-boiled eggs instead of raw eggs. Add capers, minced cornichons, minced egg white and 3 to 4 tablespoons minced fresh herbs.

REMOULADE SAUCE: Add 1/2 teaspoon anchovy paste to the recipe above for Sauce Tartare.

HERB MAYONNAISE: Add 4 to 5 tablespoons minced fresh herbs to the recipe for regular mayonnaise.

AIOLI: Soak 1 slice dry white bread in 3 tablespoons milk. Add 4 to 8 mashed garlic cloves and pound into a paste. Add the eggs to this paste and continue with the recipe for regular mayonnaise, using olive oil.

Lemon Caper Mayonnaise

6 tablespoons mayonnaise
2 teaspoons capers
1/2 teaspoon grated lemon zest
1/2 teaspoon lemon juice
1/4 teaspoon freshly ground black pepper
1/8 teaspoon crushed red pepper

Combine the mayonnaise, capers, lemon zest, lemon juice, black pepper and crushed red pepper in a small bowl and mix well. Chill until serving time.

Yield: 4 servings

Pecan-Crusted Tilapia

$1/2$ cup all-purpose flour
$1/2$ cup buttermilk
2 teaspoons hot red pepper sauce
$1/2$ cup bread crumbs
2 tablespoons finely chopped pecans
$1/2$ teaspoon salt
$1/2$ teaspoon garlic powder
$1/2$ teaspoon pepper
4 (6-ounce) tilapia fillets
2 tablespoons olive oil

Place the flour in a shallow dish. Combine the buttermilk and hot red pepper sauce in another shallow dish. Combine the bread crumbs, pecans, salt, garlic powder and pepper in a third shallow dish. Coat each tilapia fillet with the flour. Dip in the buttermilk mixture and coat with the bread crumb mixture. Sauté the fillets in the olive oil in a large skillet sprayed with nonstick cooking spray over medium-high heat for 3 minutes on each side or until the fish flakes easily.

Yield: 4 servings

TIP: Unless you have an extra-large skillet, you may find it more convenient to cook the fish in two batches, using one tablespoon olive oil to sauté three fillets at a time. Keep the first batch in a warm oven while cooking the remaining fillets.

Roasted Sea Bass with Chive Couscous and Warm Tomato Vinaigrette

TOMATO VINAIGRETTE
2 garlic cloves, minced
2 tablespoons olive oil
1 cup chopped tomato
1 green onion, cut into 3-inch pieces
and julienned
2 tablespoons fresh lemon juice
1 tablespoon sherry vinegar
1/2 teaspoon kosher salt

CHIVE COUSCOUS
1 1/4 cups chicken broth
1 tablespoon fresh lemon juice
1/4 teaspoon kosher salt
2/3 cup uncooked couscous
1/4 cup chopped fresh chives

FISH
4 (6-ounce) sea bass or halibut
fillets (about 1 1/2 inches thick)
1/4 teaspoon kosher salt
1/4 teaspoon freshly ground pepper
8 (1/4-inch-thick) lemon slices, halved
Whole chives (optional)

For the tomato vinaigrette, sauté the garlic in the olive oil in a large nonstick skillet over medium-high heat for 30 seconds or until the garlic begins to brown. Add the tomato and green onion. Cook over medium heat for 1 minute. Remove from the heat and stir in the lemon juice, sherry vinegar and salt. Keep warm.

For the couscous, combine the chicken broth, lemon juice and salt in a saucepan. Bring to a boil. Stir in the couscous and chopped chives gradually. Let stand, covered, for 5 minutes. Fluff with a fork. Cover and keep warm.

For the sea bass, season the fish with the salt and pepper. Arrange the fillets in a 7×11-inch baking dish coated with nonstick cooking spray. Place 4 halved lemon slices on each fillet. Bake in a preheated 350-degree oven for 2 minutes or until the fish flakes easily. Serve each fillet on a bed of the couscous and top with the vinaigrette. Garnish with whole chives.

Yield: 4 servings

Crab Cakes

2 tablespoons butter	Kosher salt and pepper to taste
2 tablespoons olive oil	8 ounces lump crab meat
1 cup diced celery	1/2 cup dry bread crumbs
1/2 cup diced red bell pepper	1/2 cup mayonnaise
1/2 cup diced yellow bell pepper	1 tablespoon mustard
1/2 cup diced red onion	2 eggs, beaten
1/4 cup flat-leaf parsley, chopped	Butter for frying
1 teaspoon Worcestershire sauce	Olive oil for frying
1 1/2 teaspoons hot red pepper sauce	

Heat 2 tablespoons butter and 2 tablespoons olive oil in a skillet. Add the celery, bell peppers, onion, parsley, Worcestershire sauce, hot red pepper sauce, salt and pepper. Sauté for 15 minutes or until the vegetables are tender. Cool completely. Combine the crab meat, bread crumbs, mayonnaise, mustard and eggs in a bowl and mix well. Stir in the celery mixture. Chill, covered, for 1 hour. Shape by tablespoonfuls into round patties. Fry in a little butter and olive oil in a skillet over medium heat until golden brown on both sides. Drain on paper towels.

Yield: 6 servings

TIP: For the best crab cakes, use top-quality crab meat. Atlantic blue crab, usually labeled "jumbo lump," is best. Use fine crumbs to bind the crab cakes; they won't overwhelm the flavor. Use the minimum amount of bread crumbs; you want to taste the crab, not the binder. Chilling the crab cakes before frying them will keep them from falling apart.

New Zealand Green-Lipped Mussels with Tuscan Cream Sauce

This recipe was provided by the Executive Chef of the Shedd Aquarium.

2 tablespoons butter
20 to 25 green-lipped mussels
1/2 red onion, julienned (about 1 cup)
1/3 cup julienned sun-dried tomatoes
6 kalamata olives, pitted and chopped
1 tablespoon chopped garlic
1 cup white wine
1 cup heavy cream
1/4 cup grated Parmesan cheese
1 tablespoon julienned fresh basil
1 teaspoon chopped fresh tarragon

Melt the butter in a straight-sided sauté pan or a brazier with a lid over medium-high heat. Add the mussels. Sauté for 3 to 4 minutes. Add the onion, tomatoes, olives and garlic and sauté for 3 minutes longer. Stir in the wine. Cook, covered, for 4 minutes, allowing the wine to reduce. Add the cream, cheese, basil and tarragon. Cook for 3 minutes longer.

Yield: 2 servings

Grilled (Broiled) Calamari

This recipe was provided by the Executive Chef of The Erie Café.

Geisha squid, cleaned, drained and sliced into rings
Olive oil
Whole garlic cloves
Lemon juice
Sliced jalapeño chiles
Salt and pepper
Paprika
Fresh parsley
Garlic cloves, minced
Red wine
Clam juice
Lobster base
Whipped butter

Dry the squid rings on paper towels. Combine olive oil, garlic, lemon juice, jalapeño chiles, salt, pepper, paprika and parsley in a shallow dish and mix well. Add the squid and marinate in the refrigerator overnight. Sauté minced garlic in a little olive oil. Add some red wine and simmer until the wine reduces. Stir in some clam juice and lobster base. Remove the calamari rings to a roasting pan. Grill or broil until opaque. Add the red wine sauce and broil until hot and browned, adding some whipped butter about two-thirds of the way through the cooking. Squeeze some lemon juice over the top and garnish with additional fresh parsley.

Yield: variable

THE ERIE CAFÉ

Located along the North Branch of the Chicago River on Erie Street, The Erie Café serves prime aged steaks, chops, and house specialties in a classic club-like environment.

Formerly with Club Gene & Georgetti, E. J., Larry, Ron Lenzi Jr. and Sr., grandsons and son-in-law of its founder and former owner, Gene Michelotti, now bring generations of classic Chicago steakhouse management experience to the reestablished historic Erie Café. One of the family members is always there to take care of you. Situated in the historic River North area, this architecturally significant building features arched stone windows overlooking Chicago's Loop. It was carefully renovated to become the Erie Café steakhouse and opened its doors in September 1994.

Herb-Baked Scallops

2 pounds bay scallops, rinsed and
drained on paper towels
1/2 cup (1 stick) butter
3 tablespoons minced parsley
1 1/2 teaspoons basil, crumbled
1 teaspoon kosher salt
1/4 teaspoon pepper
1/2 teaspoon minced garlic

Arrange the scallops in a single layer in a shallow 1 1/2-quart baking dish. Dot with the butter. Sprinkle with the parsley, basil, salt and pepper. Bake in a preheated 350-degree oven for 5 minutes. Add the garlic and stir the scallops to coat with the butter mixture. Bake for 20 minutes longer or until tender.

Yield: 6 servings

TIP: Try serving the scallops over slices of fresh tomatoes with basil. For a special presentation, serve the scallops in their shells.

Jambalaya

1 pound andouille, chorizo or other
smoked sausage, cut into
1/4-inch slices
2 tablespoons vegetable oil
2 cups chopped onions
3/4 cup chopped bell pepper
3/4 cup chopped celery
Salt and cayenne pepper to taste
1 cup white or brown rice
1 (14-ounce) can whole tomatoes,
chopped, with juice

2 cups water (use 1 1/2 cups for
a drier jambalaya)
1 tablespoon chopped garlic
4 bay leaves
1/4 teaspoon thyme
1 pound medium shrimp, peeled
and deveined
1/4 cup chopped green onions

Brown the sausage in the oil in a large-cast iron Dutch oven over medium heat. Add the onions, bell pepper, celery, salt and cayenne pepper. Sauté for 6 to 8 minutes or until tender and golden. Add the rice and stir to coat evenly. Add the tomatoes, water, garlic, bay leaves and thyme. Cook, covered, over medium heat for 20 minutes. Season the shrimp with salt and cayenne pepper. Add to the rice mixture. Cook for 10 minutes or until the rice is tender, the liquid is absorbed and the shrimp is pink. Let stand for 5 minutes. Remove the bay leaves. Stir in the green onions.

Yield: 6 servings

ANDOUILLE is a Cajun smoked pork sausage, traditionally flavored with salt, pepper, and garlic. It is slowly smoked (eight hours at 175 degrees) over pecan wood and sugar cane.

CHORIZO is a Spanish-style pork sausage. All versions contain roasted red peppers (pimento) and Spanish paprika for flavor and color. True Spanish chorizo is fermented and cured and can be sliced and eaten without further cooking. Try it in place of ground beef or turkey in burger recipes for an added kick, or slice and fry chorizo in olive oil and serve with deep-fried eggs for a traditional Spanish breakfast.

Fresh Asparagus with Vinaigrette

1 large bunch asparagus, trimmed
Kosher salt to taste
2 egg yolks
1 teaspoon Dijon mustard
4 tablespoons wine vinegar
$1/2$ teaspoon minced garlic
$1/2$ tablespoon chopped anchovy fillets
$2/3$ cup extra-virgin olive oil
Freshly ground pepper to taste
$1/3$ cup chopped roasted red bell pepper (optional)
$1/2$ cup freshly grated Parmesan cheese

Cook the asparagus in salted water to cover in a large skillet for 6 to 8 minutes or until tender; drain and remove to a serving dish. Whisk the egg yolks, mustard, wine vinegar, garlic and anchovies together in a bowl. Add the olive oil slowly, whisking constantly. Season with salt and pepper. Pour over the asparagus. Garnish with the bell pepper and sprinkle with the cheese.

Yield: 4 servings

TIP: If you are concerned about using raw egg yolks, use yolks from eggs pasteurized in their shells, which are sold at some specialty food stores, or use an equivalent amount of pasteurized egg substitute.

Cuban Black Beans and Rice

1 pound (2 cups) dried black beans, sorted and rinsed
1 large onion, chopped (1 cup)
1 large bell pepper, chopped (1^1/$_2$ cups)
1 (14-ounce) can diced tomatoes
5 cups water
2 tablespoons extra-virgin olive oil
2 teaspoons finely chopped jalapeño chile
5 garlic cloves, finely chopped
2 bay leaves
4 teaspoons cumin
1 teaspoon salt
Pepper to taste
3 cups hot cooked rice

Combine the black beans, onion, bell pepper, tomatoes, water, olive oil, jalapeño chile, garlic, bay leaves, cumin, salt and pepper in a 3- to 6-quart slow cooker. Cook on High for 6 to 8 hours or until the beans are tender and most of the liquid is absorbed. Remove the bay leaves. Serve over the rice.

Yield: 6 servings

CHICAGO-STYLE HOT DOG

A hot dog in this city is a steamed or boiled all-beef, natural-casing hot dog on
a poppy seed bun. It may be topped with mustard, onion, sweet pickle relish, a dill pickle spear,
tomato slices or wedges, sport peppers, and a dash of celery salt—but no ketchup.
Chicago-style hot dogs with all the toppings are sometimes said to be "dragged through the garden"
because of the unique combination of condiments. Chicagoans traditionally shun ketchup
because of the belief that ketchup is redundant in the presence of sweet pickle relish.

Zucchini Soufflé

3 cups thinly sliced zucchini
1 cup baking mix
1/2 cup finely chopped onion
1 cup grated Parmesan cheese
1/2 cup vegetable oil
1 garlic clove, finely chopped (optional)
4 eggs, lightly beaten
2 tablespoons chopped fresh parsley
1/2 teaspoon oregano
1 teaspoon seasoned salt
1/2 teaspoon salt
Dash of pepper

Combine the zucchini, baking mix, onion, cheese, oil, garlic, eggs, parsley, oregano, seasoned salt, salt and pepper in a large bowl and mix well. Pour into a greased 9×13-inch baking dish. Bake in a preheated 350-degree oven for 25 minutes or until golden brown. Cut into twenty-four 1-inch pieces.

Yield: 24 small servings

STORING FRUITS AND VEGGIES

When you store uncut tomatoes, peaches, or melons in the refrigerator, the low temperature stops the flow of natural sugars inside the
fruit, and they will have less flavor when eaten. Cut fruits need to be refrigerated, but leave the uncut ones in a paper bag on the counter.

Espresso Chocolate Walnut Brownies

This recipe needs to be chilled before serving.

3/4 cup chopped walnuts
3/4 cup all-purpose flour
1/4 cup baking cocoa
3/4 teaspoon baking powder
1/4 teaspoon kosher salt
2 tablespoons finely ground espresso beans
3 ounces unsweetened chocolate, finely chopped
3/4 cup (1 1/2 sticks) unsalted butter, softened
1 1/2 cups sugar
3 eggs, lightly beaten
1 tablespoon vanilla extract

Toast the walnuts in a single layer on a baking sheet in a preheated 350-degree oven for 6 to 8 minutes or until lightly browned. Cool completely. Sift the flour, baking cocoa, baking powder and salt together into a small bowl. Stir in the ground espresso beans. Melt the chocolate and butter in a double boiler over simmering water, stirring until smooth. Remove from the heat and stir in the sugar. Beat in the eggs and vanilla. Add the flour mixture and stir just until mixed. Stir in the toasted walnuts. Pour into a 9×13-inch baking pan lined with foil and sprayed with nonstick cooking spray. Bake in a preheated 350-degree oven for 30 to 35 minutes or until a crust forms and the center is still moist. Cool in the pan on a wire rack. Chill for 2 hours. Cut into small bars.

Yield: 24

Sweet Mandy B's Famous Cupcakes

This recipe was provided by Sweet Mandy B's Bakery.

1^1/2 cups all-purpose flour
1 cup baking cocoa
1^1/4 teaspoons baking powder
1^1/4 teaspoons baking soda
1 teaspoon salt
2 cups sugar
^{3}/4 cup hot water
^{3}/4 cup milk
2 eggs
^{1}/2 cup vegetable oil
1^1/2 teaspoons vanilla extract
Chocolate Frosting (at right)

Sift the flour, baking cocoa, baking powder, baking soda and salt together into a mixing bowl. Stir in the sugar. Turn on the mixer to medium and add the water, milk, eggs, oil and vanilla. Beat until smooth. Fill twelve foil-lined muffin cups ^{1}/2 full. Place the muffin tray on a baking sheet. Bake in a preheated 325-degree oven for 30 minutes or until a wooden pick inserted in the center comes out clean. Remove to a wire rack to cool completely. Spread Chocolate Frosting over the cupcakes.

Yield: 12 cupcakes

Chocolate Frosting

1 cup (2 sticks) butter, softened
3 tablespoons dark corn syrup
1 teaspoon vanilla extract
Pinch of salt
^{2}/3 cup baking cocoa
1 (1-pound) package confectioners' sugar
^{1}/2 cup whipping cream

Cream the butter in a mixing bowl until light and fluffy. Beat in the corn syrup, vanilla and salt. Add the baking cocoa with the machine turned off. Beat slowly until incorporated. Add the confectioners' sugar ^{1}/3 at a time, beating well after each addition. Add the whipping cream and beat until fluffy.

Yield: frosting for 12 cupcakes

Black Bottom Banana Cream Pie

Chill before serving.

1 unbaked (9-inch) pie shell	$^1/_4$ teaspoon salt
1 tablespoon cornstarch	2 eggs
2 tablespoons sugar	1 tablespoon butter
2 tablespoons baking cocoa	2 teaspoons vanilla extract
Dash of salt	3 ounces cream cheese, softened
$^1/_3$ cup milk	5 cups sliced bananas
1 ounce semisweet chocolate, chopped	(about 5 large bananas)
2 tablespoons cornstarch	1$^1/_2$ cups heavy whipping cream
1 cup milk	$^1/_4$ cup confectioners' sugar
$^1/_2$ cup sugar	Chocolate curls (optional)

Bake the pie shell in a preheated 375-degree oven until light brown. Combine 1 tablespoon cornstarch, 2 tablespoons sugar, the baking cocoa and a dash of salt in a small heavy saucepan. Whisk in $^1/_3$ cup milk gradually. Cook over medium-low heat for 2 minutes. Stir in the chocolate. Bring to a boil over medium heat. Reduce the heat to low. Cook for 1 minute, stirring constantly. Spread in the baked pie shell. Whisk 2 tablespoons cornstarch, 1 cup milk, $^1/_2$ cup sugar, $^1/_4$ teaspoon salt, the eggs and butter together in a heavy saucepan over medium heat. Bring to a boil. Reduce the heat to low. Cook for 30 seconds or until thick, stirring constantly. Remove from the heat and stir in the vanilla. Beat the cream cheese in a small bowl for 30 seconds or until light. Add $^1/_4$ cup of the hot custard and stir just until blended. Stir in the remaining custard.

Arrange the banana slices over the chocolate layer in the pie shell. Spoon the custard evenly over the bananas. Press plastic wrap onto the surface of the custard. Chill for 4 hours. Remove the plastic wrap. Whip the heavy whipping cream in a medium bowl until soft peaks form. Fold in the confectioners' sugar. Spread evenly over the custard. Garnish with chocolate curls. Chill until serving time.

Yield: 8 servings

Marvelous Mocha Pie

PIE
20 Oreo cookies, crushed
1/4 cup (1/2 stick) butter, melted
1 quart coffee ice cream, softened

CHOCOLATE SAUCE
3 ounces unsweetened
chocolate, melted
1/4 cup (1/2 stick) butter

2/3 cup sugar
2/3 cup evaporated milk
1 teaspoon vanilla extract

TOPPING
1 cup heavy whipping cream, whipped
Sliced or slivered almonds, toasted
Kahlúa (optional)

For the pie, combine the crushed cookies and butter in a small bowl and mix well. Press onto the bottom and up the side of a 9-inch pie plate. Spread the ice cream over the crust. Freeze until firm.

For the sauce, bring the chocolate, butter and sugar to a boil in a saucepan over medium heat, stirring constantly. Stir in the evaporated milk slowly. Cook until thickened, stirring constantly. Cool completely. Stir in the vanilla. Spread the sauce over the pie and return to the freezer until the sauce sets.

For the topping, spread the whipped cream over the pie. Sprinkle with almonds. Spoon a little Kahlúa over each serving.

Yield: 8 servings

VARIATIONS: Try combining different ice cream flavors and different toppings to vary the flavor of this pie. Some examples:

CHOCOLATE ICE CREAM WITH RASPBERRY PUREE: Purée the desired amount of berries in a food processor. Strain and add sugar and kirsch (optional) to taste.

VANILLA ICE CREAM WITH CARAMEL: To make the caramel sauce, heat the desired amount of sugar with 1/2 cup water in a saucepan until the sugar is dissolved, stirring constantly with a wooden spoon. Cook until the mixture turns a golden brown. Remove from the heat and stir in some heavy whipping cream or butter 1 tablespoon at a time, until the desired color and consistency is reached. Cool before assembling the pie.

Brown Sugar Pecan Pie

1 cup packed brown sugar
1/2 cup granulated sugar
1 teaspoon all-purpose flour
2 eggs, beaten
2 tablespoons milk
1 teaspoon vanilla extract
1/2 cup (1 stick) butter, melted
1 cup pecan halves
1 unbaked (9-inch) pie shell

Combine the brown sugar, granulated sugar, flour, eggs, milk and vanilla in a bowl and mix well. Add the butter and mix well. Stir in the pecans. Pour into the pie shell. Bake in a preheated 325-degree oven for 50 to 60 minutes or until a knife inserted in the center comes out clean. Cool completely before serving.

Yield: 8 servings

Chocolate Praline Cheesecake Pie

1/4 cup (1/2 stick) butter
24 pecan halves, chopped
16 ounces cream cheese, softened
1 cup packed light brown sugar
1/3 cup baking cocoa
3 eggs, beaten
1 teaspoon vanilla extract
1 (9-inch) chocolate crumb pie shell, or any other crust
12 pecan halves (optional)
Whipped cream (optional)

Melt the butter in a skillet over medium heat. Add the chopped pecans and stir until golden brown; drain on a paper towel. Beat the cream cheese and brown sugar in a bowl until light and fluffy. Beat in the baking cocoa. Add the eggs and vanilla and mix well. Stir in the toasted pecans. Pour into the pie shell. Bake in a preheated 400-degree oven for 10 minutes. Reduce the heat to 300 degrees. Bake for 30 minutes longer or until a knife inserted in the center comes out clean. Cool completely. Chill in the refrigerator for 6 hours or longer before serving. Garnish with 12 pecan halves and serve with whipped cream.

Yield: 10 to 12 servings

Cherry Cheesecake

CRUST
2¹/₂ cups graham cracker crumbs
1 cup finely chopped pecans
¹/₂ cup sugar
¹/₂ cup (1 stick) butter, melted
1 teaspoon cinnamon

FILLING
16 ounces cream cheese, softened
2 eggs
1 cup sugar
1 teaspoon vanilla extract
1 can cherry pie filling

For the crust, combine the graham cracker crumbs, pecans, sugar, butter and cinnamon in a bowl and mix well. Reserve ¹/₄ cup of the crumb mixture. Press the remaining crumb mixture onto the bottom and 1 inch up the side of a 9-inch springform pan. Bake in a preheated 350-degree oven for 10 minutes. Cool on a wire rack.

For the filling, beat the cream cheese in a mixing bowl until soft. Add the eggs and beat until smooth. Beat in the sugar and vanilla. Pour into the cooled crust. Sprinkle with the reserved crumb mixture. Bake in a preheated 375-degree oven for 20 to 25 minutes. Cool in the pan. Spread the cherry pie filling over the cheesecake. Chill for 8 to 10 hours before serving.

Yield: 8 to 10 servings

Chocolate Soufflé

5 ounces semisweet chocolate
3 tablespoons water
4 egg yolks
6 tablespoons sugar
¹/₂ teaspoon cinnamon
6 egg whites
Pinch of salt
4 tablespoons sugar to coat the dishes
Vanilla ice cream (optional)

Melt the chocolate with the water in a saucepan over low heat or in a microwave-safe bowl in a microwave. Beat the egg yolks and 6 tablespoons sugar in a mixing bowl until pale and creamy. Stir in the melted chocolate and cinnamon. Beat the egg whites and salt in a mixing bowl until stiff peaks form. Fold the egg whites ¹/₂ at a time into the chocolate mixture. Sprinkle 1 tablespoon sugar in each of four greased ramekins, shaking to coat the bottom and side. Spoon the soufflé batter into the ramekins, peaking the batter above the top of each dish. Bake in a preheated 425-degree oven for 10 to 12 minutes. Serve immediately with a side of vanilla ice cream.

Yield: 4 servings

TIP: The ice cream can also be melted and poured over the warm soufflés as a sauce.

Mixed Berries with Berry Coulis

COULIS	BERRY MIXTURE
1/2 cup fresh or thawed frozen raspberries	1 cup fresh raspberries
1/2 cup fresh or thawed frozen blueberries	1 cup fresh blueberries
1/2 cup fresh or thawed frozen blackberries	1 cup fresh blackberries
2 tablespoons water	2 tablespoons dark brown sugar
2 1/2 teaspoons sugar	1/4 teaspoon grated orange zest
	1/4 teaspoon orange flower water (optional)
	Sprigs of mint (optional)

For the coulis, combine the raspberries, blueberries, blackberries, water and sugar in a food processor and process until smooth. Strain through a fine sieve into a bowl; discard the solids. Chill, covered, until serving time.

For the berries, combine the raspberries, blueberries and blackberries in a large bowl. Add the brown sugar, orange zest and orange flower water and toss gently. Chill, covered, until serving time.

To serve, spoon the coulis into individual serving dishes. Top with the berry mixture. Garnish with mint sprigs.

Yield: 6 to 8 servings

TIP: Serve this dessert with a scoop of ice cream or a dollop of crème fraîche.
To make your own crème fraîche, combine 1 cup sour cream with
1 to 2 cups heavy cream (do not use ultra-pasteurized cream) in a bowl and
mix well. Let stand at room temperature for several hours or until
thickened. Cover and store in the refrigerator.

Italian Dolce

1 (8-ounce) bar German's sweet chocolate
6 tablespoons brewed espresso
12 tablespoons sugar
6 egg yolks
1 quart heavy whipping cream

Heat the chocolate in a double boiler or in a saucepan over hot water, stirring until melted. Add the espresso and keep warm. Beat the sugar and egg yolks together in a mixing bowl. Fold the chocolate mixture into the sugar mixture. Whip the whipping cream in a mixing bowl until stiff peaks form. Fold into the chocolate mixture. Chill for at least 4 hours (preferably overnight) before serving.

Yield: 6 servings

TIP: If you are concerned about using raw egg yolks, use yolks from eggs pasteurized in their shells, which are sold at some specialty food stores, or use an equivalent amount of pasteurized egg substitute.

Baked Caramel Popcorn

1 cup (2 sticks) butter
2 cups packed brown sugar
$1/2$ cup light corn syrup
1 teaspoon salt
$1/2$ teaspoon baking soda
1 teaspoon vanilla extract
6 quarts popped popcorn

Melt the butter in a saucepan. Stir in the brown sugar, corn syrup and salt. Bring to a boil, stirring constantly. Boil for 5 minutes without stirring. Remove from the heat and stir in the baking soda and vanilla. Pour gradually over the popcorn in a large bowl, stirring constantly. Spread in two large shallow baking pans. Bake in a preheated 250-degree oven for 1 hour, stirring every 15 minutes. Cool completely. Break into pieces and store in a tightly covered container.

Yield: 6 to 8 servings

TIP: For a different flavor, add a little amaretto to the caramel.

VARIATION: CHEESE POPCORN: Pop two 3-ounce bags of microwave popcorn using the package directions. Melt $1/4$ cup ($1/2$ stick) butter in a saucepan and drizzle over the popcorn. Sprinkle with $1/2$ to $3/4$ cup grated Parmesan cheese and toss to coat.

Decadent Chocolate Toffee

2 cups sugar
1 cup water
1 cup (2 sticks) unsalted butter
8 ounces milk chocolate chips
1 tablespoon shortening
Crushed toppings such as pecans,
macadamia nuts or peppermint candies
8 ounces white chocolate chips
1 tablespoon shortening

Combine the sugar and water in a saucepan. Bring to a boil. Add the butter 1 stick at a time. Bring back to a boil. Reduce the heat to medium. Cook to 300 degrees on a candy thermometer, stirring frequently. Pour into a 9×13-inch baking pan. Chill in the refrigerator for 30 minutes. Break the toffee into small pieces. Melt the milk chocolate chips with 1 tablespoon shortening in a double boiler or in a saucepan over hot water, stirring until smooth. Dip $1/2$ of the toffee pieces in the chocolate mixture. Coat with crushed toppings of your choice. Repeat the process with the white chocolate chips and 1 tablespoon shortening. Chill the pieces on waxed paper in the refrigerator for 30 minutes.

Yield: 20 to 30 pieces

TIP: For a richer chocolate flavor, substitute semisweet chocolate for the milk chocolate. This is a great winter snack or holiday giveaway.

Brandied Orange Shells

3 to 4 cups water
2 cups sugar
4 very large navel oranges,
   cut into halves crosswise
Sugar for coating

2 cups brandy
$1/2$ gallon vanilla ice cream
8 candied lemon leaves or mint leaves
   (optional)

Combine the water and sugar in a saucepan just large enough to hold the oranges. Heat until the sugar is dissolved. Add the oranges; add more water if necessary to barely cover them. Simmer gently for 20 to 30 minutes or until very tender. Let stand overnight. Stir in the brandy. Chill the oranges in the brandy syrup in tightly covered jars or plastic containers for 3 days or up to 3 months.

To serve, scoop the pulp carefully from the orange shells. Purée the pulp in a blender or food processor, adding enough of the brandy syrup to reach a sauce consistency. Dry the shells and coat them with sugar several times. Place them cut side down between coatings. Fill the shells with vanilla ice cream and top with the orange sauce. Garnish with the candied lemon leaves or mint leaves. (Both the shells and the filling may be eaten.)

Yield: 8 servings

TIP: Add chocolate sauce if desired for a different look and taste.

FRESH FRUIT FOR A LIGHTER DESSERT

PEELED AND SKINNED GRAPEFRUIT SECTIONS broiled with a brown sugar topping

MELON BALLS with lemon juice and fresh mint leaves

BANANAS baked with honey, orange liqueur, and thyme, and sprinkled with confectioners' sugar

PEARS poached in white wine and pepper, topped with chocolate
fudge sauce and crème fraîche

FRESH FIGS, walnuts, crystallized ginger, and crème fraîche

RASPBERRIES or STRAWBERRIES marinated in balsamic vinegar and sugar
for 2 to 3 hours

FALL

Some consider fall in Chicago to be one of the best times of the year; it's a season of both tradition and change.

Besides the start of the school year, Chicagoans can always count on Oktoberfest, the Chicago Marathon,

Halloween, and Bears football, among other rich traditions. And with change in the air, we watch the brilliant leaves

of autumn fall as our city's parks and trees prepare for the wintry days ahead.

FALL

FALL MENUS

AFTER-THEATER SUPPER

24-Hour Cocktail, 101

Portobellos with Caramelized Onions
and Brie, 104

Apple-Stuffed Pork Tenderloin, 117

Parmesan Twice-Baked Potatoes, 126

Vanilla Ice Cream with
Warm Butterscotch Sauce, 127

There has always been a thriving theater scene here in Chicago. Famous theaters such as Steppenwolf, Second City, and the Chicago Theatre have bred stars such as Dan Akroyd, John Malkovich, and Gary Sinese. Chicago is proud to offer year-round theater options from pre-Broadway viewings to quality plays in small neighborhood venues.

The Chicago Symphony Orchestra is one of the world's most renowned. Their best-selling recordings win prestigious awards, and their syndicated radio broadcasts are heard by millions nationwide. Since 1891, the orchestra has given over 630 premiers.

Orchestra Hall—This great hall was designed by Chicago Symphony Orchestra trustee and Chicago architect Daniel Burnham and completed in 1904.

Lyric Opera—The Civic Opera Building, home to the Lyric Opera, is the second largest opera Auditorium in North America, with a seating capacity of 3,563.

HALLOWEEN CELEBRATION

Harvest Butternut Squash Soup, 111

Baked Brie with Apples
and Cranberries, 103

Pork Chops with Parmesan
Sage Crust, 115

Wild Rice Pilaf, 115

Taffy Apple Salad, 107

Caramel Pecan Pie, 127

Chicago has something to offer for the entire family at Halloween time. For a real scare, attend one of the city's haunted ghost tours, which go through some of Chicago's most famous haunted places. Or, take kids to the Daley Center for Chicagoween Pumpkin Plaza. The Chicago Park District also has pumpkin patches, hayrides, and haunted houses throughout the area.

MARATHON DINNER "PASTA PARADE"

Brie and Basil Linguini, 119

Pasta with Sausage and Escarole, 119

Penne with Ricotta and Pine Nuts, 120

Pan-Seared Chicken with Artichokes
and Pasta, 121

Pasta with Basil, Arugula and
Walnut Pesto, 122

Thai Chicken Linguini, 122

Gnocchi with Pork and Tomato
Gorgonzola Sauce, 123

Everyday Lasagna, 124

The Chicago Marathon is held annually in early October. Nearly 40,000 runners from all over the world compete and experience a scenic tour of Chicago, passing through various Chicago neighborhoods and many area landmarks as they run. The marathon ends a summer running season filled with shorter training runs, ranging in length from 5Ks to half-marathons, sponsored by different Chicago-based charities.

24-Hour Cocktail

12 lemons, halved
8 cups water
1 1/2 cups sugar
1 fifth or 1 quart smooth whiskey
Pinch of salt

Squeeze the lemons, reserving the juice and twelve of the lemon rind halves. Bring the water and sugar to a boil in a saucepan. Cook until the sugar is dissolved, stirring constantly. Stir in the lemon juice. Add the lemon rinds. Remove from the heat and stir in the whiskey and salt. Strain through a fine sieve into bottles. Chill in the refrigerator for 24 hours before serving.

Yield: 3 quarts

Consume with good stories to tell.

French Toast Baked with Bananas

1/4 cup (1/2 stick) butter, melted
8 (1/2-inch-thick) slices French bread
2 tablespoons sugar
1/2 teaspoon cinnamon
3 eggs
3/4 cup orange juice or tangerine juice
4 bananas, sliced
Toasted pecans

Pour the melted butter into a baking pan large enough to hold the bread slices in one layer. Arrange the bread slices in the butter. Combine the sugar and cinnamon in a bowl and sprinkle over the bread. Whisk the eggs and orange juice together in a shallow dish. Dip each bread slice in the egg mixture for 15 seconds on each side. Return the bread to the baking pan. Pour the remaining egg mixture over the top. Layer the banana slices over the bread. Bake in a preheated 425-degree oven for 10 minutes. Turn the bread and bake for 10 minutes or until puffed and golden brown. Sprinkle with toasted pecans.

Yield: 4 servings

Oven-Baked German Apple Pancakes

This recipe was provided by the Executive Chef of the Yelton Manor Bed and Breakfast.

3/4 cup all-purpose flour
3/4 cup milk
3 eggs
Pinch of nutmeg
4 tablespoons butter
2 large Granny Smith apples, thinly sliced
Confectioners' sugar to taste
Syrup

Mix the flour, milk, eggs and nutmeg in a bowl just until moistened; the batter will be a little lumpy. Heat 2 tablespoons butter in each of two 9-inch pie plates in a preheated 425-degree oven until very hot. Divide the batter equally between the pans. Top with the apple slices. Bake for 15 to 18 minutes or until brown. Sprinkle with confectioners' sugar and serve with your favorite syrup.

Yield: 2 servings

OKTOBERFEST

Every fall the German-American Festival gives Chicagoans the opportunity to celebrate Oktoberfest. This event is full of good foods, beer, music, and dancing. The festival has been held for more than eighty years and takes place in one of Chicago's old German neighborhoods: Lincoln Square. The event is fun for the entire family.

FROM ELIZABETH'S KITCHEN

I have made this Pumpkin Bread hundreds, perhaps thousands, of times. My grandmother, Mrs. Mark Twain (Margaret Arnold) Swearengen, created it about fifty years ago. My grandmother, whom we call M. A., is ninety-three years old and still going very strong, taking great care of my grandfather, who is also ninety-three. They live in Monroe City, Missouri, where my family has lived for generations. This recipe is a family staple. I bake and give dozens of loaves as gifts at holiday time. Although it is called bread, it is really more of a cake.

Pumpkin Bread

3 cups sugar
1 cup canola oil
3 eggs
1 (15-ounce) can pumpkin
3 1/3 cups all-purpose flour
1 teaspoon baking soda
1/2 teaspoon baking powder
1 teaspoon each ground cloves, cinnamon and nutmeg
1/2 teaspoon salt
1/2 to 1 cup chopped walnuts (optional)

Beat the sugar and oil in a large mixing bowl until creamy. Add the eggs and beat well. Stir in the pumpkin. Combine the flour, baking soda, baking powder, cloves, nutmeg, cinnamon and salt. Add to the pumpkin mixture, stirring just until mixed. Stir in the walnuts. Pour into a greased and floured bundt or tube pan, two 7×9-inch loaf pans, three 4×8-inch loaf pans or four 3×7-inch loaf pans. Bake in a preheated 350-degree oven for 1 1/4 hours for the bundt pan, 1 hour for the large loaf pans or 45 minutes for the smaller loaf pans or until a wooden pick inserted in the center comes out clean and the top begins to crack.

Yield: 8 servings

Oatmeal Muffins

2 cups rolled oats
1 3/4 cups milk
1 3/4 cups all-purpose flour
1/2 cup packed light brown sugar
1 tablespoon baking powder
1/2 teaspoon kosher salt
1/4 teaspoon cinnamon
3 eggs, lightly beaten
1/2 cup (1 stick) unsalted butter or
margarine, melted
1 teaspoon vanilla extract
3/4 cup packed light brown sugar
1/4 teaspoon cinnamon

Combine the rolled oats and milk in a bowl. Let stand for 10 minutes. Combine the flour, 1/2 cup brown sugar, the baking powder, salt and 1/4 teaspoon cinnamon, making a well in the center. Stir in the liquid ingredients and the oatmeal mixture just until combined, being careful not to overmix. Batter may be lumpy. Fill twelve greased muffin cups 3/4 full. Combine 3/4 cup brown sugar and 1/4 teaspoon cinnamon in a bowl and crumble over the batter. Bake in a preheated 400-degree oven for 16 to 18 minutes or until light golden or a wooden pick inserted in the center comes out with crumbs attached; do not overbake.

Yield: 12 muffins

VARIATION: Add fruit to your muffins for extra flavor. Use 1/2 to 3/4 cup of fresh or dried fruit; adjust the amount depending on how much moisture is in the fruit.

Baked Brie with Apples and Cranberries

1/2 cup chopped apple
1/4 cup sliced almonds
1/4 cup dried cranberries
1 tablespoon brown sugar
1 tablespoon butter, melted
1 (8-ounce) round Brie cheese

Combine the apples, almonds, cranberries and brown sugar in a bowl and mix well. Stir in the melted butter. Cut the cheese in half horizontally. Spread half the apple mixture over the cut side of one cheese round. Top with the second round cut side down. Spoon the remaining apple mixture over the top. Bake in a preheated 350-degree oven for 12 to 15 minutes or until the cheese is soft.

Yield: 8 servings

TIP: This autumnal appetizer also works well throughout the winter months.

Portobellos with Caramelized Onions and Brie

3 red onions, sliced
2 tablespoons olive oil
3 tablespoons balsamic vinegar
1 tablespoon brown sugar
Leaves from 4 sprigs fresh thyme
Salt and freshly ground pepper to taste
8 medium or 4 large portobello
mushroom caps
Olive oil for brushing
1 small wheel or medium wedge Brie cheese,
cut into thin slices

Cook the onions in 2 tablespoons olive oil in a skillet over low heat until caramelized, drizzling the balsamic vinegar and sprinkling the brown sugar gradually over the onions during the cooking. Add the thyme, salt and pepper when the onions just begin to caramelize. Brush the mushroom caps with olive oil and place in a baking pan. Bake in a preheated 400-degree oven for 10 minutes or just until softened. Fill the mushroom caps with the caramelized onions and top with slices of the cheese. Broil for 2 to 3 minutes or until the cheese is melted and golden brown.

Yield: 4 to 8 servings

TIP: Roquefort is a good alternative to Brie and provides a richer taste in this dish.

Asiago Cheese Dip

1/2 cup sun-dried tomatoes
1 cup hot water
1 cup mayonnaise
1 cup sour cream
1/2 cup (2 ounces) shredded asiago cheese
1/2 cup chopped fresh mushrooms
1/4 cup chopped green onions
1 teaspoon asiago cheese

Soak the tomatoes in the water in a small bowl; drain and squeeze out excess water. Slice the tomatoes into strips. Combine the tomato strips, mayonnaise, sour cream, 1/2 cup cheese, the mushrooms and green onions in a bowl and mix well. Spoon into a pie plate or baking dish to be used as a serving dish. Sprinkle with 1 teaspoon cheese. Bake in a preheated 350-degree oven for 25 minutes.

Yield: 8 to 10 servings

Neiman Marcus Dip

1 cup (4 ounces) shredded
  Cheddar cheese
3 slices bacon, crisp-cooked
  and crumbled
1/2 cup mayonnaise
1/4 cup chopped almonds
1 tablespoon chopped green onion

Combine the cheese, bacon, mayonnaise, almonds and green onion in a bowl and mix well.

Serve with crackers.

Yield: 1 1/2 cups

RUNNING IN CHICAGO

Chicago is considered to be one of the best cities in the United States for runners. The city boasts over twenty miles of lakefront pathway on which to run. A not-for-profit advocacy group was founded in 1978, in the year following the first Chicago Marathon, called Chicago Area Runner's Association (CARA). It has grown to be one of the largest running organizations in the Midwest and the third largest in the nation, with 9,000 members. CARA works tirelessly with the Chicago Park District to maintain the running paths and serves as the official training sponsor for the Chicago Marathon. The success rate of its training program, designed by the renowned marathoner Hal Higdon, is that 99 percent of the trainees make it to the starting line each year. Ask around; if a Chicagoan hasn't run the marathon, he or she knows someone who has.

Beef, Mushroom and Cheese Ball

1 (4-ounce) can mushroom stems and
  pieces, drained
1 can black olives, drained and chopped
1 bunch green onions, cut into 2- to
  3-inch pieces
2 (1/2-ounce) packages chipped beef
8 ounces cream cheese, softened
1 teaspoon bourbon
1/2 teaspoon seasoned salt

Process the mushrooms, olives, green onions and chipped beef in a food processor until smooth. Remove to a mixing bowl. Add the cream cheese, bourbon and seasoned salt and mix well. Shape into a ball and wrap in plastic wrap. Chill in the refrigerator overnight.

Serve with assorted crackers.

Yield: 16 servings

TIP: Chipped beef is available at your grocery store in the deli section.

Chicken Puffs

2 cups shredded boiled, boneless skinless chicken breast
1 cup mayonnaise
1/2 to 3/4 cup grated fontina or Gruyère cheese
1/2 cup freshly grated Parmesan cheese
2 large shallots, minced
1/4 teaspoon basil
1/4 teaspoon thyme
Pinch of salt and pepper
1 loaf pumpernickel or rye party-size bread, toasted
1/4 cup freshly grated Parmesan cheese

Combine the chicken and mayonnaise in a large bowl. Combine the fontina cheese, 1/2 cup Parmesan cheese, the shallots, basil, thyme, salt and pepper in a bowl and mix well. Add to the chicken mixture and mix well. Arrange the toasted bread on a baking sheet. Top each toast with a heaping spoonful of the chicken mixture. Sprinkle with 1/4 cup Parmesan cheese. Bake in a preheated 350-degree oven for 10 to 12 minutes or until the top is lightly browned and the bread is crunchy. Serve immediately.

Yield: 10 to 12 servings

MIXED GREENS

Enjoy a variety of greens in your next salad. Here are some choices available in your market:

AMARANTH—green leaves with purple centers, earthy taste.

ARUGULA—bright green, long and tender leaves with a spicy flavor. Old arugula is more bitter than baby arugula.

BELGIAN ENDIVE—small compact white, greenish, and yellowish leaves. The whiter the leaves, the less bitter the taste.

BIBB LETTUCE—smaller version of romaine with sweet leaves but less watery; firmer and crunchier than Boston lettuce.

BOSTON LETTUCE—fragile, slippery outer leaves surround a compact core.

CHRYSANTHEMUM—thin spiky leaves usually used in stir-fries. Fragrant and pine-flavored. Its petals are also edible.

DANDELION GREENS— pleasant chewy texture and slightly bitter flavor. Usually sold in large, dark green bunches.

ESCAROLE—dense, chewy, and bitter. In Italy it is usually cooked, especially in soups.

FRISEE/CURLY ENDIVE—dark green curly leaves with a crispy texture and bitter taste.

GREEN LEAF LETTUCE— Delicate, floppy, crinkled leaves with a mild flavor.

Crispy Garlic Bread

1 to 2 loaves bread, thinly sliced
3/4 cup (1 1/2 sticks) butter, melted
2 tablespoons minced garlic
6 to 8 ounces shredded Parmesan cheese
Dried dill weed seasoning

Cut 2-inch rounds from each slice of bread, using a biscuit cutter or glass. Combine the butter and garlic in a small bowl and brush generously over the bread slices. Sprinkle the cheese and dill weed over the top. Place on a baking sheet. Bake in a preheated 350-degree oven for 10 minutes or until golden. Serve immediately.

Yield: 6 to 8 servings

Spinach and Cranberry Salad

1 bag fresh spinach
4 ounces feta cheese, crumbled
1 cup dried cranberries
2 cups sliced almonds
Balsamic vinaigrette to taste

Combine the spinach, cheese, cranberries and almonds in a salad bowl. Add the vinaigrette and toss gently.

Yield: 8 servings

MORE MIXED GREENS

ICEBERG LETTUCE—compact heads often served in chunks or to add crunch to a salad.

MÂCHE—soft fuzzy leaves with a mild flavor.

MIZUNA—flat, long, spiky leaves with an intense mustard-radish flavor.

RADICCHIO—small compact head of reddish purple, striped with white. Its bitter, yet mild-flavored leaves are used in salads for color.

RED LEAF LETTUCE—similar to green leaf lettuce, but with red-tipped leaves.

ROMAINE—long green heads with crunchy leaves and a refreshing sweet taste. Perfect for heartier dressings.

SORREL—dark, deep-green leaves with a sweet-sour, tart taste. For a milder flavor, remove the stems.

TATSOI—long stems and flat green leaves with a bitter taste.

WATERCRESS—bright green petal-like leaves and thin stems with a sharp, peppery, mustardy flavor.

LOLLO ROSA—curly leaves with reddish edges. Similar to red and green leaf lettuce, but firmer and crisper.

Taffy Apple Salad

1 (8-ounce) can crushed pineapple, drained, juice reserved
1 egg
1/3 cup sugar
2 tablespoons cider vinegar
1 tablespoon all-purpose flour
4 cups bite-size pieces peeled Delicious apples
8 ounces whipped topping
1 cup salted dry-roasted peanuts, finely chopped

Combine the pineapple juice, egg, sugar, cider vinegar and flour in a saucepan and mix well. Cook over medium heat until thickened, stirring constantly. Chill in the refrigerator for 1 hour. Combine the pineapple, apples, whipped topping and half of the peanuts in a serving bowl and mix well. Stir in the chilled sauce. Top with the remaining peanuts.

Yield: 6 servings

Black Bean Salad

1 (15-ounce) can black beans
1/2 cup (2 ounces) shredded
  Monterey Jack cheese
1 tablespoon chopped fresh cilantro
2 cups cooked rice, at room temperature
1/2 cup low-fat Italian salad dressing
Salt and pepper to taste

Combine the beans, cheese and cilantro in
a salad bowl. Add the rice and salad dressing
and mix well. Season with salt and pepper.

Yield: 4 servings

MAKE YOUR OWN FLAVORED OILS

Heat olive oil with flavorings
such as herbs, spices, and
garlic. You can use the flavored
oil instead of plain olive oil
or other vegetable oil for
cooking, or you can purée the
oil with the ingredients used
for flavoring and use as a
topping. Here are a few possible
flavorings for 1 cup olive oil:

GARLIC: 1 head roasted garlic

CHILI: 1/2 shallot, 1/2 head
garlic, 1/2 teaspoon cayenne
pepper, 1/2 teaspoon paprika,
3/4 teaspoon cumin,
1/2 teaspoon red pepper flakes

CUMIN: 1/4 cup cumin seeds

CURRY: 3/4 tablespoon curry
powder, 1/2 shallot, 1/2 teaspoon
fennel seeds, 1/2 teaspoon
whole peppercorns

LEMON: zest of 6 lemons
(or limes, oranges,
grapefruits, and so forth)

GINGER: 1/3 cup chopped
peeled ginger

HERBS: 2 tablespoons
fresh herbs

Parmesan and Arugula Orange Salad

2 large bunches arugula, trimmed of
  large stems
1/4 cup extra-virgin olive oil
Fresh lemon juice to taste
1 teaspoon kosher salt
1 teaspoon freshly ground pepper
1 teaspoon kosher salt
8 ounces Parmesan cheese, shaved into
  thin strips
3 blood oranges, peeled and sectioned

Wash the arugula leaves and remove any
large stems. Dry thoroughly and set aside.
Whisk the olive oil, lemon juice, 1 teaspoon
salt and the pepper together in a bowl.
Sprinkle the remaining 1 teaspoon salt over
the arugula leaves in a salad bowl. Add the
cheese, blood oranges and dressing and
toss gently. Arrange the salad on individual
plates with the oranges on top.

Yield: 6 servings

Yukon Gold Potato Salad with Prosciutto and Truffle Oil

This salad can be made up to two hours ahead.

2 pounds Yukon Gold potatoes, peeled and
cut into $1/4$-inch-thick slices
$2^1/2$ cups low-sodium chicken broth
2 tablespoons butter
3 ounces chopped sliced prosciutto
1 cup chopped celery
$1/2$ cup chopped sweet onion (such as Vidalia)
$1/2$ cup chopped fresh chives
1 tablespoon (or more) truffle oil
1 tablespoon fresh lemon juice
Salt and pepper to taste

Combine the potatoes and chicken broth in a large saucepan. Bring to a boil. Reduce the heat and simmer, partially covered, for 6 minutes or just until the potatoes are tender. Remove the potatoes from the broth to a large bowl. Boil the broth for 13 minutes or until reduced to $1/3$ cup. Pour over the potatoes and toss gently until the broth is absorbed. Melt the butter in a nonstick skillet over medium heat. Add the prosciutto and sauté for 6 minutes or until crisp. Add the sautéed prosciutto, celery, onion and chives to the potato mixture and mix gently. Whisk the truffle oil and lemon juice together in a small bowl. Drizzle over the potato mixture and toss gently. Season with salt, pepper and additional truffle oil if desired. Serve warm or at room temperature.

Yield: 6 servings

Mushroom Soup

2¹/2 tablespoons extra-virgin olive oil
1 tablespoon butter
1¹/2 pounds sliced mushrooms, including
at least 12 ounces wild mushrooms
¹/2 cup chopped shallots
3 tablespoons dry sherry
5 tablespoons all-purpose flour
1 teaspoon dried thyme,
or 1 tablespoon fresh thyme
4¹/2 cups chicken stock
1 teaspoon salt
³/4 teaspoon pepper
Chopped fresh parsley (optional)

Heat the olive oil and butter in a soup pot over high heat until the butter is melted. Add the mushrooms and shallots. Cook for 5 minutes or until the mushrooms are wilted. Stir in the sherry, flour and thyme. Reduce the heat to low. Cook for 5 minutes, stirring constantly to deglaze the pan. Stir in the chicken stock, salt and pepper. Simmer for 20 minutes or until slightly thickened.Ladle into warm bowls and garnish with chopped fresh parsley.

Yield: 4 to 6 servings

A TASTE OF PARMESAN

True Parmigiano-Reggiano has small white crystals that result from the ripening period—24 months on average. The taste is delicate, fragrant, and very savory.

If you are feeling adventurous, here are a few good substitutes:

GRANA PADANO—the name *Grana* was popularly bestowed upon the cheese because of its "grainy" consistency. Like Parmigiano-Reggiano, it is a cooked, semi-fat hard cheese. The aged version, Stravecchio Oro del Tempo, also contains the white crystals found in Parmigiano-Reggiano.

ARGENTINE REGGIANITO—Saltier than Parmigiano-Reggiano. This cheese was originally produced in Argentina by Italian immigrants, who tried to create a Parmigiano-Reggiano using local ingredients.

PECORINO ROMANO—Stronger in taste and saltier than Parmigiano-Reggiano; it is a sheep's milk cheese.

PIAVE VECCHIA—Use this cheese for a richer, buttery taste. It has butterscotch and caramel flavors and is sweeter and nuttier than Parmesan. This cheese is new to the American market and may be difficult to find.

Roasted Onion Soup

This recipe was provided by chef/owner Bruce Sherman of North Pond.

3 sweet onions, such as Vidalia or
Walla Walla, quartered
1 yellow onion, quartered
4 garlic cloves
3 tablespoons canola oil
¹/2 teaspoon salt
¹/4 teaspoon white pepper
1 carrot, finely chopped
1 rib celery, finely chopped
1 shallot, thinly sliced
1 cup whipping cream
6 cups chicken broth or vegetable broth
6 tablespoons unsalted butter, cubed
Salt and white pepper to taste
Herbed croutons (optional)
Freshly grated Parmesan cheese

Toss the onions and garlic with the canola oil, ¹/2 teaspoon salt and ¹/4 teaspoon pepper in a large roasting pan, stirring to coat the vegetables. Roast in a preheated 375-degree oven for 40 minutes, stirring every 10 minutes. Add the carrot, celery and shallot. Roast for 10 minutes. Stir in the cream. Roast for 10 minutes longer. Remove the pan to the cooktop and add 5 cups of the broth. Bring to a boil. Reduce the heat and simmer for 10 minutes. Purée the soup in a blender in batches or with an immersion blender. Add the butter and stir until smooth. Press the purée through a sieve. Stir in some of the remaining 1 cup broth to thin if necessary. Add more salt and pepper as desired. Serve hot with herbed croutons and Parmesan cheese.

Yield: 6 servings

Harvest Butternut Squash Soup

1 (3-pound) butternut squash, peeled, seeded and cut
into 1-inch cubes
2 tablespoons olive oil
Salt and pepper to taste
1 tablespoon butter
1 tablespoon olive oil
1 large yellow onion, diced
(about 1 1/2 cups)
3 ribs celery, chopped (about 1 1/2 cups)
1 tablespoon chopped fresh sage
(about 6 large leaves)
6 cups chicken broth
1/2 cup freshly grated or slivered
Parmesan cheese

Toss the squash with 2 tablespoons olive oil in a baking pan. Season generously with salt and pepper. Roast in a preheated 400-degree oven for 15 minutes. Turn the cubes. Roast for 15 minutes longer or until caramelized. Heat the butter and 1 tablespoon olive oil in a Dutch oven or large stockpot over medium heat. Add the onion, celery and sage. Cook for 10 minutes or until tender, stirring occasionally. Add the squash, chicken broth and more salt and pepper if desired. Simmer for 30 minutes or until the liquid is flavorful. Process in batches in a blender or food processor until smooth. Return the soup to the pan and keep warm. Top servings with the cheese and serve with fresh bread.

Yield: 6 servings

Beef Barley Soup

7 cups water
3 (10-ounce) cans condensed beef broth
1 pound stew meat, cut into
1/2-inch chunks
2 large onions, chopped
1 pound sliced mushrooms
4 carrots, sliced
1 (14-ounce) can diced tomatoes, drained
1/2 teaspoon salt
1/2 teaspoon pepper
1 cup quick-cooking pearl barley

Combine the water, beef broth, stew meat, onions, mushrooms, carrots, tomatoes, salt and pepper in a soup pot. Bring to a boil. Reduce the heat and simmer for 20 minutes. Add the barley and simmer for 15 to 20 minutes longer or until the barley is tender.

Yield: 8 servings

Fricassee de Pollo

1/3 cup extra-virgin olive oil
1 whole chicken, cut into serving pieces
1 red bell pepper, chopped
1 onion, chopped
3 garlic cloves, chopped
1 cup tomato salsa (not paste)
1/2 cup capers
1/4 teaspoon pepper
1 cup chicken stock
1 cup white wine
Hot cooked rice
Roasted red pepper or pimento (optional)
Chopped green or black olives (optional)

Heat the olive oil in a skillet over medium-high heat. Brown the chicken in the oil on both sides; remove to a dish. Add the bell pepper, onion and garlic to the skillet. Cook for 5 minutes or until the vegetables are tender. Add the chicken, salsa, capers, pepper and chicken stock. Simmer, covered, for 15 minutes. Add the white wine and simmer until the sauce is thickened and the chicken tests done. Serve over rice. Garnish with roasted red pepper or pimento and chopped green or black olives. (Rinse the green olives before adding.)

Yield: 4 servings

FRICASSEE

This term is used to describe a dish of meat (usually chicken) that has been sautéed before being stewed with vegetables. The end result is a thick, chunky stew, often flavored with wine.

Whole Roasted Baby Chicken with Potato Gnocchi, Honey-Glazed Parsnips and Young Beets

This recipe was provided by the Executive Chef of Naha.

1 small organic chicken	1 pound beets
Salt and cracked black pepper to taste	2 to 4 parsnips
Several sprigs fresh thyme	2 tablespoons honey
2 tablespoons olive oil	1 pound ready-to-cook gnocchi
6 tablespoons butter	1 to 2 tablespoons extra-virgin
1 1/4 cups white wine	olive oil (optional)

Season the chicken with salt and pepper. Stuff the thyme into the chicken. Truss the chicken with clean cotton string or kitchen twine. Heat 2 tablespoons olive oil in a heavy sauté pan. Add the chicken and cook until browned all over, turning occasionally. Remove to a roasting pan. Dot with 1 tablespoon of the butter. Roast in a preheated 350-degree oven for about 1 hour. Remove the chicken and let stand until cool. Pour the wine into the roasting pan and reserve the juices. Cut the chicken into smaller pieces, discarding the bones.

Cook the beets in cold water to cover in a large pot over medium-high heat until tender. Cool and peel the beets under running water, gently pulling off the skins by hand. (Wear plastic gloves to avoid stains.) Trim the bottom and top of the beets and cut them into halves or wedges, depending on the size.

Peel the parsnips and cut them into desired shapes. Sauté the parsnips in 2 tablespoons of the butter in a skillet. Remove to a roasting pan and roast in a preheated 350-degree oven for about 10 minutes or until tender. Drizzle with the honey. Roast for 10 minutes or until glazed and caramelized.

Boil the gnocchi in water using the package directions. Melt the remaining 3 tablespoons butter in a large sauté pan and sauté the gnocchi for 15 minutes.

To assemble, place the chicken on an ovenproof serving plate. Surround the chicken with the sautéed gnocchi. Top with the glazed parsnips and beets. Reheat in the oven. Drizzle with the extra-virgin olive oil or with the reserved pan juices.

Yield: 4 servings

Chicken Manhattan

1 egg
3/4 cup Italian-style bread crumbs
4 boneless skinless chicken breasts,
pounded to 1/4-inch thickness
2 tablespoons extra-virgin olive oil
1/2 cup chopped onion
2 tablespoons butter
1/2 pound mushrooms, sliced
1 garlic clove, minced
1 (10-ounce) package frozen chopped
spinach, thawed and squeezed dry
1/2 teaspoon nutmeg
4 slices provolone cheese
1/2 cup dry white wine

Beat the egg lightly in a shallow dish. Pour the bread crumbs into another shallow dish. Dip the chicken breasts in the egg and coat with the bread crumbs. Sauté the chicken in the olive oil in a skillet for 4 minutes on each side or until lightly browned. Remove from the heat; cover and keep warm. Sauté the onion in the butter in another skillet over medium heat for 2 minutes or until almost tender. Add the mushrooms and garlic. Sauté for 2 to 5 minutes or until tender. Stir in the spinach and nutmeg. Cook until heated through. Spoon 1/4 of the spinach mixture over each chicken breast in the first skillet. Arrange the provolone slices over the spinach mixture. Add the wine. Cook, covered, for 5 minutes or until the cheese is melted and the chicken is tender and cooked through.

Yield: 4 servings

Sautéed Chicken over Wilted Spinach with Orange Sauce

2 boneless chicken breasts (about 1 pound)
Salt and pepper to taste
1 tablespoon unsalted butter
1 tablespoon olive oil
1 large shallot, thinly sliced
2 tablespoons sugar
1 orange, cut crosswise into thin slices and seeded
1/3 cup water
3 tablespoons white wine vinegar
1/8 teaspoon hot red pepper flakes
1 tablespoon chopped fresh parsley
4 cups packed spinach leaves (about 1 bunch)

Season the chicken breasts with salt and pepper. Sauté skin side down in the butter and olive oil in a skillet over medium-high heat for 5 minutes or until the skin is crisp and golden. Turn the chicken. Sauté for 5 minutes or just until cooked through. Remove the chicken to a plate and keep warm.

Add the shallot to the skillet. Cook for 1 minute, stirring frequently. Sprinkle the sugar over the shallot. Cook without stirring until the sugar is melted and the shallot is golden. Add the orange slices, water, white wine vinegar and hot red pepper flakes. Simmer until the sugar is dissolved. Add the parsley and salt to taste. Simmer for 1 minute longer or until the sauce is thickened to the desired consistency. Remove 2/3 of the sauce to a small bowl. Add the spinach to the remaining sauce and season with salt to taste. Turn the spinach in the sauce just until wilted. Divide the spinach between two plates and top each with a chicken breast. Spoon the sauce over the chicken.

Yield: 2 servings

Pork Chops with Parmesan Sage Crust

3/4 cup freshly grated Parmesan cheese
2 eggs
1 cup Italian-style bread crumbs
1 tablespoon dried sage
1 teaspoon grated lemon zest
4 center cut pork loin chops
Kosher salt and freshly ground pepper to taste
3 tablespoons olive oil

Place the cheese in a shallow dish. Whisk the eggs in another shallow dish. Combine the bread crumbs, sage and lemon zest in a third shallow dish. Season the pork chops with salt and pepper. Coat with the cheese. Dip the chops in the eggs. Coat with the bread crumb mixture. Heat the olive oil in a large skillet over medium heat. Add the pork chops. Cook for 7 to 10 minutes per side or until the crust is golden brown and the chops reach 160 degrees on a meat thermometer.

Yield: 4 servings

MORE TASTE OF PARMESAN

SAP SAGO—Made in Switzerland and also known as schabziger, this is a hard, pungent cheese flavored with clover.

VEZZENA STRAVECCHIO—Medium-bodied with a peppery finish, it is made from partially skimmed cow's milk and has a sharp flavor and crumbly, flaky texture.

MYZITHRA—A Greek cheese similar in texture to ricotta salata, it has a nutty flavor and cottony texture.

WHAT IS WILD RICE?

Wild rice is the seed of a wild aquatic grass, native to Minnesota and other Great Lakes states. The longer grain means that the rice will have a better quality. Accurate cooking time is important, because undercooked wild rice is difficult to chew and overcooked wild rice is gluey. Simmer the rice slowly until tender, checking for doneness every few minutes after the first thirty-five minutes. Use chicken broth to soften the rice's flavor; if the rice is still too strong for your taste, mix it with some long grain white rice.

Wild Rice Pilaf

1 package wild rice mix
2 cups water
1/2 cup (1 stick) butter
1 large can sliced mushrooms
1 small onion, diced
1/2 small red bell pepper, diced
1/4 cup chopped almonds
1/2 cup chopped celery

Cook the wild rice mix in the water using the package directions. Combine the butter, undrained mushrooms, onion, bell pepper, almonds and celery in a saucepan. Bring to a boil, stirring constantly. Reduce the heat and simmer for 30 minutes or until the liquid has evaporated. Stir in the rice mixture. Spoon into a greased baking dish. Bake, covered, in a preheated 350-degree oven for 30 minutes or until heated through.

Yield: 4 servings

TIP: Sliced fresh mushrooms can be used instead of canned mushrooms.

Thai Curried Shrimp with Peppers

1 onion, thinly sliced	1 cup water
2 tablespoons olive oil	1 red bell pepper, thinly sliced
2 garlic cloves, minced	1 yellow bell pepper, thinly sliced
1 tablespoon finely chopped peeled fresh ginger	1 cup unsweetened coconut milk (use light coconut milk if desired)
1 to 2 tablespoons red curry paste	2 tablespoons white wine vinegar
2 tomatoes, seeded and chopped	24 large shrimp, peeled and deveined

Sauté the onion in the olive oil in a skillet for 7 to 10 minutes or until light golden brown. Add the garlic and ginger. Sauté for 2 minutes or until tender. Stir in the curry paste. Cook for 2 to 3 minutes or until the paste begins to stick to the bottom of the pan, stirring constantly. Add the tomatoes and water. Simmer over medium-low heat for 20 minutes or until the tomatoes are very tender, stirring occasionally. Add the bell peppers, coconut milk and white wine vinegar. Bring to a simmer and add the shrimp. Cook over low heat for 5 minutes or just until the shrimp are cooked through.

Yield: 4 servings

TIP: Canned red curry paste is available in the Asian/Thai section of well-stocked supermarkets or at Asian-operated grocery stores.

THAI CURRIES

Thai curry powder is a blend of spices, with the exact ingredients and proportions varying. It usually contains turmeric, coriander, cumin, fenugreek, ginger, nutmeg, fennel, cinnamon, cardamom, cloves, and pepper. Different brands range in taste from mild to hot, depending on the amount and type of pepper used.

Red curry paste is a mixture of dry chili pepper, shallot, garlic, galangal, lemon grass, cilantro root, peppercorn, coriander, salt, shrimp paste, and kaffir lime zest.

118

Brie and Basil Linguini

4 tomatoes, cut into 1/2-inch cubes
1 pound Brie cheese, rind removed and
    cheese torn into irregular pieces
1 cup fresh basil leaves, cut into strips
3 garlic cloves, finely minced
1 cup olive oil
1/2 teaspoon salt
1/2 teaspoon pepper
6 quarts water
1 1/2 pounds linguini
1 tablespoon olive oil
2 teaspoons salt
Pepper to taste
Freshly grated Parmesan cheese

Combine the tomatoes, Brie cheese, basil, garlic, 1 cup olive oil, 1/2 teaspoon salt and 1/2 teaspoon pepper in a large serving bowl. Let stand, covered, at room temperature for at least 2 hours. Bring the water to a boil in a large stockpot. Add the linguini, 1 tablespoon olive oil and the remaining 2 teaspoons salt. Cook for 8 to 10 minutes; drain. Add the pasta, pepper to taste and Parmesan cheese to the tomato mixture and toss to combine.

Yield: 4 servings

THE CHICAGO MARATHON

The LaSalle Bank Chicago Marathon is held in October each year, typically Columbus Day weekend. By late summer, training is well under way and hard to ignore on the weekends. Italian restaurants across the city become accustomed to groups of people "carbo-loading" on Friday nights, and drinking large amounts of water instead of wine. Saturday mornings see the lakefront path crowded with groups of runners running side by side. Cafés and diners are frequented by groups of runners afterwards, sweaty but hungry and thirsty. Appropriately, the weekend of the race, a traditional pasta dinner (see page 100) is held at the Hilton Hotel on South Michigan Avenue. Those who opt to eat out must make reservations early; the best Italian restaurants will be booked weeks in advance.

Pasta with Sausage and Escarole

2 garlic cloves, minced
    (about 1 tablespoon)
3 tablespoons extra-virgin olive oil
1 pound hot Italian sausage,
    casings removed
1 cup dry white wine
1 cup heavy cream
1/4 cup finely chopped fresh
    flat-leaf parsley
1 teaspoon finely chopped fresh rosemary
1/2 teaspoon crushed red pepper
Kosher salt and freshly ground black
    pepper to taste
1 large head escarole, stemmed and
    cut into thirds horizontally
1 pound rigatoni or other tubular pasta
Freshly grated Parmesan cheese

Cook the garlic in the olive oil in a skillet over medium heat until translucent and fragrant. Add the sausage. Cook for 5 to 7 minutes or until cooked through, stirring until crumbly. Add the wine, stirring to deglaze the pan. Add the cream, parsley, rosemary, red pepper, salt and black pepper. Bring to a simmer and add the escarole. Cook for 8 to 10 minutes or just until wilted, stirring occasionally. Cook the pasta in boiling salted water until al dente; drain. Add the pasta to the skillet. Cook for 3 minutes or until the sauce is thickened. Serve with Parmesan cheese.

Yield: 4 to 6 servings

Pasta with Basil, Arugula and Walnut Pesto

2 cups fresh basil leaves
2 cups arugula leaves
1/4 cup packed fresh flat-leaf parsley
3 tablespoons coarsely chopped walnut pieces
3 tablespoons olive oil
4 garlic cloves
3/4 cup grated Parmigiano-Reggiano cheese
1/3 cup low-sodium chicken broth
3/4 teaspoon salt
1/2 teaspoon pepper
1/4 cup pine nuts, toasted
8 cups hot cooked linguini
(about 1 pound uncooked pasta)

Combine the basil, arugula, parsley, walnuts, olive oil and garlic in a food processor. Pulse seven or eight times or until the mixture forms a paste. Add the cheese, chicken broth, salt, pepper and pine nuts. Pulse until well mixed. Toss the pesto with the hot linguini in a large serving bowl.

Yield: 6 servings

MORE PASTA SHAPES

LASAGNA—large flat noodles, about 3 inches wide

LINGUINI—thin, flat, solid strands, about 1/8 inch wide

MACARONI/DUMPLING—thin tubular pasta in various widths and lengths

MANICOTTI—thick ridged tubes; may be cut straight or at an angle

ORECCHIETTE/EARS—smooth curved rounds of flat pasta, about 1/2 inch in diameter

ORZO/BARLEY—small grain-shaped pasta

PASTINA—tiny pasta in a variety of shapes, including stars, rings, and alphabets

BASIL BASICS

Known as a tomato's best friend, basil is also a delicious herb for seasoning chicken, fish, pasta, stews, salads, and vegetables. Add fresh basil during the last ten minutes of cooking as heat dissipates its flavor quickly.

Thai Chicken Linguini

1 cup mild or medium picante sauce
1/4 cup chunky peanut butter
2 tablespoons honey
2 tablespoons orange juice
1 teaspoon soy sauce
1/2 teaspoon ginger
3 boneless skinless chicken breasts, cut into strips
2 tablespoons vegetable oil
8 ounces linguini, cooked
Fresh cilantro
Peanuts
Red bell pepper, thinly sliced

Combine the picante sauce, peanut butter, honey, orange juice, soy sauce and ginger in a saucepan over low to medium heat and mix well. Cook until smooth, stirring constantly. Sauté the chicken in the oil in a skillet over medium to high heat for 5 minutes. Stir in 1/4 cup of the peanut sauce. Add the chicken and remaining sauce to the cooked linguini and toss well. Serve with cilantro, peanuts and red bell pepper strips.

Yield: 4 servings

TIP: For a seafood version of this dish, substitute shrimp for the chicken.

Gnocchi with Pork and Tomato Gorgonzola Sauce

4 tablespoons olive oil
$1/2$ pound pork tenderloin, diced
8 dried black olives, pitted and diced
4 garlic cloves, minced
Gorgonzola cheese to taste, cut into 2-inch cubes
Freshly ground pepper
$1/4$ teaspoon sage
$1/2$ cup dry marsala
1 (28-ounce) can ground tomatoes
1 pound gnocchi, cooked

Heat a wok until very hot. Add the olive oil and pork and stir-fry until the pork begins to brown. Add the olives and garlic. Stir-fry until the pork is thoroughly browned. Add the cheese, 8 twists of pepper and the sage. Cook until the cheese is almost melted, stirring constantly. Add the marsala and stir to deglaze the pan. Stir in the tomatoes. Cook until heated through.

Serve over the hot gnocchi.

Yield: 4 servings

MAKE YOUR OWN POTATO GNOCCHI

Peel, cook, and mash the desired amount of potatoes. The best way to mash is with a ricer; lumps in the mashed potatoes will make the gnocchi fall apart when cooked.

Add to the potatoes enough flour to make a dough that is not sticky and that will roll easily. The moisture level of potatoes varies, so there is no exact ratio. You have to gauge the amount of flour to add by the stickiness of the dough.

Work the dough by hand just until it comes together, but no longer.

Parmesan Twice-Baked Potatoes

2 baking potatoes, baked and
 halved lengthwise
1/4 cup mayonnaise or sour cream
1/4 cup grated Parmesan cheese
2 tablespoons butter

2 tablespoons milk
Salt and pepper to taste
1/4 cup crumbled crisp-cooked bacon
 (optional)
1/4 cup chopped chives (optional)

Scoop the baked potato pulp from the shells into a mixing bowl, reserving the shells. Add the mayonnaise, cheese, butter, milk, salt, pepper, bacon and chives to the potatoes and mix well. Spoon into the shells. Bake in a preheated 375-degree oven for 20 minutes or until golden brown.

Yield: 4 servings

TIP: Let the baked potatoes cool slightly before removing the pulp. Keep the shells in the oven while making the filling to prevent them from becoming soggy.
OTHER FILLINGS: Cheddar cheese and scallions; chipotle chiles and onions; Indian spices and peas; Monterey Jack cheese and pesto; pepper jack cheese and bacon; smoked salmon and chives; bacon, cabbage, and Cheddar cheese; broccoli, Cheddar cheese, and scallions; ham, peas, and Gruyère cheese

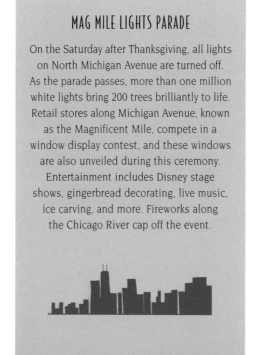

MAG MILE LIGHTS PARADE

On the Saturday after Thanksgiving, all lights on North Michigan Avenue are turned off. As the parade passes, more than one million white lights bring 200 trees brilliantly to life. Retail stores along Michigan Avenue, known as the Magnificent Mile, compete in a window display contest, and these windows are also unveiled during this ceremony. Entertainment includes Disney stage shows, gingerbread decorating, live music, ice carving, and more. Fireworks along the Chicago River cap off the event.

Skillet Cookie

This recipe was provided by the Executive Chef of the Four Corners Restaurant.

6 to 7 ounces cookie dough
3 scoops vanilla ice cream
2 tablespoons chocolate syrup
2 tablespoons caramel sauce
Heavy whipping cream, whipped

Grease a 7-inch cast-iron skillet. Press the dough evenly onto the bottom of the skillet. Bake in a preheated 400-degree oven for 10 minutes or until golden brown. Top the hot cookie with the ice cream, chocolate syrup, caramel sauce and whipped cream. Serve immediately.

Yield: 4 servings

Vanilla Ice Cream with Warm Butterscotch Sauce

1 cup heavy cream
1¼ cups hard dark butterscotch candies or toffee candies, finely chopped
Vanilla ice cream

Bring the cream to a boil in a saucepan over medium-high heat. Stir in the butterscotch. Reduce the heat to medium. Cook until the candy is melted, stirring constantly. Cool slightly.

Serve over the ice cream.

Yield: 6 servings

THE GREAT CHICAGO FIRE

The Great Chicago Fire of 1871 that destroyed much of the city has long been blamed on Mrs. Kate O'Leary's cow kicking over a lamp. In 1997, the Chicago City Council, after looking into the matter, passed a resolution exonerating Mrs. O'Leary and her cow. The real culprit may never be known, but at least we now know that Kate and her cow were innocent.

Caramel Pecan Pie

1 (1-crust) pie pastry
28 caramels
¼ cup (½ stick) butter
¼ cup water
¾ cup sugar
2 eggs
½ teaspoon vanilla extract
¼ teaspoon salt
1½ cups coarsely chopped pecans, toasted

Fit the pie pastry into a 9-inch pie plate. Fold under the edge and crimp. Prick the bottom and side with a fork. Bake in a preheated 400-degree oven for 6 to 8 minutes or until lightly browned. Remove to a wire rack to cool completely. Combine the caramels, butter and water in a large saucepan over medium heat. Cook for 5 to 7 minutes or until melted and smooth, stirring constantly. Remove from the heat. Combine the sugar, eggs, vanilla and salt in a bowl and mix well. Add to the caramel mixture and mix well. Stir in the pecans. Pour into the pie shell. Bake in a preheated 400-degree oven for 10 minutes. Reduce the heat to 350 degrees. Bake for 20 to 25 minutes or until a knife inserted in the center comes out clean.

Yield: 8 servings

TIP: Pie pastry keeps for up to six months in the freezer as long as it is tightly wrapped in foil or freezer wrap and sealed in a freezer bag. Freezing pie pastry in the pie plate is even more convenient. You don't even need to thaw it before baking. Just add a little extra cooking time.

McCormick Tribune
Plaza and Ice Rink

WINTER

WINTER MENUS

"THE BEARS ARE GOING TO THE SUPER BOWL" PARTY

Baked Artichoke Dip, 139

Layered Bean Dip, 138

Texas Caviar, 141

Buffalo Chicken Dip, 141

Pimento Cheese, 142

Chicago Chili, 161

Cheese Enchilada Casserole, 160

Corn Bread

Cinnamon Cheesecake Squares, 173

The first Super Bowl was played on January 15, 1967. The Super Bowl is the second-largest U.S. food consumption day, following Thanksgiving.

The 1985 Chicago Bears team recorded the song "Super Bowl Shuffle" and were nominated for a Grammy, Best Rhythm & Blues Vocal Performance—Duo or Group, the first and only nomination for a sports team.

VALENTINE'S DAY

Valentinis, 134

Blue Cheese Chopped Salad, 142

Roasted Rack of Lamb, 149

Baked Risotto with Asparagus, Spinach and Parmesan, 163

Rich and Delicious Dessert, 174

Enjoy a Valentine's Day date ice-skating under the stars at Millennium Park's McCormick Tribune Ice Rink. Millennium Park is often considered the largest roof garden in the world, having been constructed on top of a railroad yard and large parking garages. Of its total 24.5 acres of land, Millennium Park contains 524,358 square feet of permeable area (12.04 acres). Planning for the park began in October 1997, construction began in October 1998, and it was completed in July 2004.

WINTER MENUS

HOLIDAY COCKTAIL PARTY

Baked Brie with Toasted Pecans, 139

Hot Crab Dip, 138

Roasted Pepper and Provolone Crisps, 140

Stuffed Mushrooms, 139

Beef Tenderloin with Merlot Shallot Sauce, 150

Sweet Potato Casserole, 162

Roasted Asparagus with Balsamic Browned Butter, 162

Hazelnut Gâteau, 172

Here are a few tips for the right amounts of food and drink
for your holiday party.

FOOD: For heavy to medium appetizers, plan on four to five pieces
per guest. For lighter appetizers, plan on five to six pieces per guest.

DRINKS: Wine and beer: One and a half
glasses per guest. A bottle of wine contains five glasses. For mixed
drinks, two and a half drinks per guest and for nonalcoholic
beverages, 8 ounces per guest.

ICE: One 5-pound bag per five guests

HOLIDAY COOKIE EXCHANGE

Cream Cheese Brownies, 165

Double Chocolate Cookies with Dried Cherries, 166

Junior League of Chicago's Gazebo Almond Fudge, 166

Holiday Bark, 167

Scotch Bars, 167

Toffee Bars, 168

Iced Sugar Cookies, 168

Chocolate Gingerbread Cookies, 169

Lemon Ginger Cookies, 169

Frango Mint Chocolate Cookies, 170

Each person brings a set number of the same cookies based on the
number of people doing the exchanging. They exchange cookies,
bringing home a wide variety of homemade cookies.
As the host, serve appetizers to the guests and refreshments
such as hot chocolate, hot apple cider, or coffee. Or turn the occasion
into a "workshop" where guests bring prepared dough and the
cookies and treats are baked at the gathering.

Valentinis

2 bottles Champagne
1/2 cup raspberry-flavored vodka
Raspberries (optional)

Pour the Champagne into a large pitcher. Add the vodka and mix well.

Serve in Champagne glasses. Garnish each serving with 3 or 4 raspberries.

Yield: 16 servings

TIP: Add a splash of lemon-lime soda or seltzer.

Irish Hot Chocolate

During the holidays, add a candy cane stirrer to each mug.

1/2 cup baking cocoa
1/3 cup sugar
1 teaspoon vanilla extract
1/2 cup cold water
Pinch of salt
2 1/4 cups 2% milk
3/4 cup half-and-half
1/3 to 1/2 cup Bailey's Irish cream,
  or to taste
Whipped cream
Shaved bittersweet chocolate

Whisk the baking cocoa, sugar, vanilla, water and salt together in a large heavy saucepan over low heat. Cook until the baking cocoa is dissolved and the mixture is a smooth paste, stirring constantly. Add the milk and half-and-half gradually. Simmer for 2 minutes, stirring constantly. Stir in the Bailey's Irish cream. Pour into mugs. Top with whipped cream and shaved chocolate.

Yield: 4 to 6 servings

Blueberry-Stuffed French Toast

This recipe requires overnight refrigeration.

12 slices white bread, crusts trimmed
and bread cubed
16 ounces block-style cream cheese
1 cup blueberries
12 eggs
1/3 cup maple syrup
2 cups milk

Arrange 1/2 of the bread cubes in a greased 9×13-inch baking dish. Slice the cream cheese and layer over the bread cubes. Spread the blueberries over the bread and cream cheese. Layer the remaining bread cubes over the blueberries. Whisk the eggs, maple syrup and milk together in a bowl. Pour evenly over the bread. Chill, covered with foil, overnight. Bake, covered with foil, in a preheated 350-degree oven for 30 minutes. Bake, uncovered, for 30 minutes longer.

Yield: 4 to 6 servings

Good Morning Egg Casserole

1 cup chopped green bell pepper
1 cup chopped red bell pepper
1/2 cup chopped white onion
2 cups eggs, beaten
1 cup milk
1 cup (4 ounces) shredded sharp
  Cheddar cheese
1 teaspoon Italian seasoning
1/4 teaspoon pepper
6 slices bread, torn into pieces
1/4 cup chopped green onions

Sauté the bell peppers and white onion in a greased skillet for 4 minutes or until tender. Place in a large bowl. Stir in the eggs, milk, cheese, Italian seasoning and pepper. Spread the bread pieces in a greased 2-quart baking dish. Pour the egg mixture evenly over the bread. Bake in a preheated 350-degree oven for 45 to 50 minutes or until a knife inserted in the center comes out clean. Sprinkle with the green onions.

Yield: 4 to 6 servings

Breakfast Muffins

1 (10-count) can refrigerated
buttermilk biscuits
1 (8-ounce) package sage-flavored
brown-and-serve sausage
2 tablespoons chopped onion
2 eggs
1/2 cup (2 ounces) shredded
Cheddar cheese
Salt and pepper to taste
1 egg white

Separate the buttermilk biscuits and cut each one in half. Press 1/2 biscuit into each of ten greased muffin cups. Brown the sausage and onion in a large skillet over low heat for 3 to 5 minutes, stirring until crumbly; drain. Place in a large bowl. Add the eggs, cheese, salt and pepper and mix well. Spoon 1 tablespoon into each muffin cup. Cover with the remaining biscuit halves, pressing the edges together to seal. Beat the egg white with a little water in a small bowl. Brush over each muffin top. Bake in a preheated 450-degree oven for 10 to 12 minutes or until golden brown.

Yield: 10 servings

TIP: If you wish to eliminate the eggs, substitute 1/4 cup bread crumbs, 2 tablespoons milk and 2 teaspoons Dijon mustard.

FROM ELIZABETH'S KITCHEN

These biscuits are perfect for Sunday brunch or dinner. They freeze beautifully after they are baked. A dependable biscuit recipe is a staple in any Southern cook's repertoire, even if he or she has relocated to Illinois.

Angel Biscuits

3 envelopes dry yeast
1 1/2 cups warm water
4 cups self-rising flour
1/2 teaspoon salt
1/2 cup sugar
1 cup shortening

Dissolve the yeast in the warm water. Mix the flour, salt and sugar in a bowl. Cut in the shortening until crumbly. Add the yeast mixture, mixing with a fork to form a ball. Knead on a floured surface four or five times. Roll 1/2 inch thick. Cut with a 1-inch or 1 1/2-inch biscuit cutter. Bake on a baking sheet in a preheated 400-degree oven for 8 to 10 minutes. Cool on a wire rack. Freeze in plastic freezer bags if desired.

Yield: about 20 biscuits

Serbian Nut Rolls

2 cups (4 sticks) butter, softened
1/2 cup granulated sugar
6 egg yolks
5 cups sifted all-purpose flour
1 large cake yeast

1 cup warm milk
6 egg whites
1 cup packed brown sugar
2 pounds walnuts, finely ground

Cream the butter and granulated sugar in a mixing bowl until light and fluffy. Beat in the egg yolks. Add the flour and mix well. Combine the yeast and warm milk in a small bowl, crumbling with the fingers. Stir into the flour mixture. Knead the dough on a floured surface until smooth and elastic. Place in a greased bowl, turning to coat the surface. Let rise, covered, in a warm place until doubled in bulk. Punch the dough down.

Beat the egg whites in a mixing bowl until stiff peaks form. Beat in the brown sugar gradually. Divide the dough into three equal portions. Knead one portion on a floured surface and spread with 1/3 of the egg white mixture. Sprinkle with 1/3 of the walnuts. Roll up and place on a greased baking sheet. Repeat with the remaining dough portions. Bake in a preheated 350-degree oven for 45 to 60 minutes or until brown. Cut each roll into four large pieces, or as desired.

Yield: 12 nut rolls

TIP: You can make an icing that will sweeten these rolls by combining melted butter, brown sugar, and cinnamon. Stir to dissolve the brown sugar, and then spoon the mixture over the rolls.

ABOUT SERBIANS IN CHICAGO

Chicago has a large Serbian population. There are several beautiful Serbian Orthodox churches in the area with their own distinctive architecture. Some of the oldest and most well known are open for tours year-round.

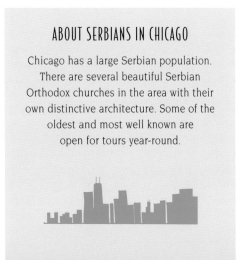

Layered Bean Dip

1 (16-ounce) can refried beans
1 (15-ounce) can black beans,
    drained and rinsed
1/2 cup sour cream
1 cup salsa
1 cup (4 ounces) shredded
Mexican-blend or sharp Cheddar cheese
Chopped fresh cilantro (optional)
Chopped green onions (optional)

Combine the refried beans and black beans in a bowl and mix well. Spread in an 8×8-inch baking dish. Layer with the sour cream, salsa and cheese. Bake, covered, in a preheated 375-degree oven for 20 minutes. Uncover and bake for 10 minutes longer or until bubbly. Garnish with chopped fresh cilantro and green onions.

Yield: 8 servings

Hot Crab Dip

8 ounces cream cheese, softened
1/4 cup grated Parmesan cheese
1/4 cup mayonnaise
1/4 cup dry white wine
2 green onions with tops, thinly sliced
1 garlic clove, finely chopped
2 tablespoons sugar
1 teaspoon dry mustard
2 (6-ounce) cans crab meat, drained
    and flaked
Grated Parmesan cheese for topping
1/3 cup sliced almonds (optional)
Paprika (optional)

Combine the cream cheese, 1/4 cup Parmesan cheese, the mayonnaise, white wine, green onions, garlic, sugar and mustard in a bowl and mix well. Stir in the crab meat. Spoon into an ovenproof serving dish. Sprinkle with additional Parmesan cheese. Bake in a preheated 375-degree oven for 15 to 20 minutes or until hot and bubbly. Cool for 5 minutes. Sprinkle with the almonds and paprika.

Yield: 8 to 10 servings

Baked Artichoke Dip

2 (8-ounce) cans artichoke hearts,
drained and chopped
1 cup mayonnaise
1 1/2 cups grated Parmesan cheese
Chopped green onions
Salt and pepper to taste

Combine the artichoke hearts, mayonnaise and cheese in a bowl and mix well. Stir in green onions to taste. Season with salt and pepper. Spoon into an ovenproof serving dish. Bake in a preheated 350-degree oven for 30 minutes. Serve hot.

Yield: 8 servings

Baked Brie with Toasted Pecans

1 (1-pound) round Brie cheese
1/2 cup chopped pecans or other
favorite nut
1/4 cup (1/2 stick) butter
1/4 cup minced fresh parsley
Crackers or French bread

Bake the Brie in an ovenproof serving dish in a preheated 300-degree oven for 10 minutes or until the cheese is soft and heated through. Toast the pecans in the butter in a skillet. Stir in the parsley. Spoon over the warmed Brie.

Serve with crackers or French bread slices.

Yield: 8 to 10 servings

GETTING TO THE HEART OF A FRESH ARTICHOKE

To get the heart of a fresh artichoke, trim the stem from the artichoke bottom. Remove the leaves, beginning at the bottom, until only the heart and cone of inner leaves are left. Cut off the cone and trim around the heart to remove all bits of green.

The trimmed artichoke heart should have a whitish color. If you are not cooking the hearts immediately, keep them in a bowl of water with lemon juice to prevent discoloration.

Stuffed Mushrooms

1 1/2 pounds mushrooms
Lemon juice for washing
1/2 cup unseasoned bread crumbs
1/3 cup grated Parmesan cheese
1/4 cup grated onion
2 garlic cloves, minced
2 tablespoons dried parsley
2 teaspoons salt
1/4 teaspoon freshly ground pepper
1/2 teaspoon oregano
2/3 cup olive oil

Wash the mushrooms in water and a little lemon juice; dry the caps and remove the stems. Combine the stems, bread crumbs, cheese, onion, garlic, parsley, salt, pepper and oregano in a food processor and process until finely chopped. Spoon the mixture into the mushroom caps. Pour a little of the olive oil into a baking pan, spreading to cover the bottom of the pan. Arrange the mushroom caps in the pan and drizzle with the remaining olive oil. Bake in a preheated 350-degree oven for 25 minutes.

Yield: 6 to 8 servings

TIP: Avoid preparing the mushrooms too early, as they darken over time.

Roasted Pepper and Provolone Crisps

2 pitas, halved horizontally to make 4 rounds
2 tablespoons olive oil
1 teaspoon paprika
$^1/_2$ teaspoon oregano
$^1/_4$ teaspoon kosher salt
1 (12-ounce) jar roasted red peppers,
drained and cut into strips
4 slices lemon
1 garlic clove, sliced
$^1/_4$ teaspoon kosher salt
2 tablespoons olive oil
1 cup (4 ounces) shredded provolone cheese

Arrange the pita rounds cut side up on a baking sheet. Brush with 2 tablespoons olive oil. Sprinkle with the paprika, oregano and $^1/_4$ teaspoon salt. Broil for 2 minutes or until crisp. Sauté the red peppers, lemon, garlic and $^1/_4$ teaspoon salt in 2 tablespoons olive oil in a skillet for 3 minutes or until the peppers are hot and fragrant. Spoon evenly over the pita rounds. Sprinkle with the cheese. Broil for 3 minutes or until the cheese is melted. Cut into strips.

Yield: 4 to 6 servings

TIP: Almost any prepared vegetable from the deli counter
can make a delicious substitute for the peppers. Try cured olives,
marinated artichoke hearts, or mushrooms.

Texas Caviar

1 (15-ounce) can white corn, drained
1 (15-ounce) can black-eyed peas,
drained and rinsed
3 tablespoons salsa
1 tomato, chopped
1 green bell pepper, chopped
1/2 onion, chopped
1/2 cup Italian salad dressing
1 tablespoon hot red pepper sauce
Handful of chopped fresh cilantro
or fresh parsley

Combine the corn, black-eyed peas, salsa, tomato, bell pepper, onion, dressing, hot red pepper sauce and cilantro in a bowl and mix well. Let stand for a few hours for the flavors to blend before serving.

Yield: 6 to 8 servings

Buffalo Chicken Dip

16 ounces cream cheese
1 (12-ounce) bottle ranch
or blue cheese salad dressing
2 cups diced celery
2 to 3 chicken breasts, cooked and shredded
1 (5-ounce) bottle hot sauce
2 cups (8 ounces) shredded Colby jack cheese

Combine the cream cheese, salad dressing and celery in a saucepan over medium-low heat. Cook until smooth, stirring constantly. Stir in the shredded chicken and hot sauce. Pour into a 9×13-inch baking dish. Sprinkle the cheese over the top. Bake in a preheated 350-degree oven for 25 minutes. Stir the melted cheese thoroughly into the dip.

Serve with crackers and celery sticks.

Yield: 15 to 20 servings

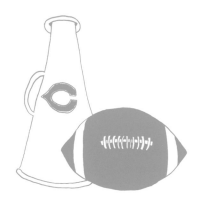

Pimento Cheese

4 cups (1 pound) shredded Cheddar cheese
1 small jar whole pimentos
1/2 cup (or more) mayonnaise
1 tablespoon pickle juice
Dash of onion powder
Dash of Tabasco sauce
Salt and pepper to taste

Combine the cheese and pimentos in a food processor and process until smooth. Add the mayonnaise and pulse until blended, adding more mayonnaise if necessary to reach the desired consistency. Add the pickle juice, onion powder, Tabasco sauce, salt and pepper and blend well.

Serve with crustless bread.

Yield: About 2 cups

Blue Cheese Chopped Salad

3 tablespoons fresh lemon juice
1/3 cup extra-virgin olive oil
Kosher salt or sea salt to taste
Freshly ground pepper to taste
6 ounces blue cheese, crumbled
1 romaine heart, chopped into 1/2-inch pieces
1 head radicchio, chopped into 1/2-inch pieces
2 heads Belgian endive, chopped into 1/2 inch pieces

Whisk the lemon juice and olive oil together in a salad bowl. Season with salt and pepper. Add the cheese, romaine, radicchio and Belgian endive and toss to combine.

Yield: 4 servings

"Company's Coming" Salad

4 tablespoons extra-virgin olive oil
3 tablespoons sherry vinegar
Salt and pepper to taste
1/2 to 1/3 cup chopped walnuts
1 head romaine, torn or sliced
2 green apples, thinly sliced
1 (11-ounce) can mandarin oranges
1/2 to 1/3 cup crumbled Gorgonzola cheese

Whisk the olive oil, vinegar, salt and pepper together in a small bowl. Add the walnuts and let stand for 30 minutes. Combine the romaine, apples, mandarin oranges and cheese in a salad bowl. Add the dressing and toss to combine. Serve immediately.

Yield: 4 servings

Endive, Avocado and Red Grapefruit Salad

2 red grapefruit
2 tablespoons honey
1 1/2 tablespoons sour cream
1 teaspoon white wine vinegar
1/4 teaspoon kosher salt
Pepper to taste
2 tablespoons extra-virgin olive oil
4 Belgian endives, halved, cored and
   cut into 1-inch pieces
1 Haas avocado, sliced

Cut the sections from the grapefruit over a bowl, allowing the sections and juices to fall into the bowl. Squeeze any remaining juice from the grapefruit into the bowl. Whisk the honey, sour cream, vinegar, salt and 4 tablespoons of the collected grapefruit juice together in a small bowl. Season with pepper. Add the olive oil in a slow stream, whisking constantly. Divide the endives and avocado among four salad plates. Drizzle each serving with 1/4 of the dressing. Top with the grapefruit sections.

Yield: 4 servings

Mrs. Hering's Famous Chicken Potpie

This recipe was provided by The Walnut Room of Marshall Field's.

The dish is best prepared with overnight refrigeration.

CHICKEN
1 (3¹/2-pound) chicken
1 carrot
1 rib celery
1 small onion, halved
2 teaspoons salt

PASTRY
1¹/2 cups all-purpose flour
¹/2 teaspoon salt
¹/2 cup (1 stick) cold unsalted
  butter, diced
¹/4 cup shortening, chilled
3 to 4 tablespoons ice water

FILLING
6 tablespoons unsalted butter
1 large onion, diced (about 1¹/4 cups)
3 carrots, thinly sliced on the diagonal
3 ribs celery, thinly sliced
  on the diagonal
¹/2 cup all-purpose flour
1¹/2 cups milk
1 teaspoon chopped fresh thyme leaves
¹/4 cup dry sherry
³/4 cup frozen green peas, thawed
2 tablespoons minced fresh parsley
2 teaspoons salt
¹/2 teaspoon freshly ground pepper
1 egg
1 tablespoon water

For the chicken, combine the chicken, carrot, celery, onion and salt in a large stockpot. Add cold water to cover. Bring to a boil over high heat. Reduce the heat and simmer for 45 minutes. Place the chicken on a plate and set aside. Increase the heat to high. Boil the broth for 20 minutes; strain through a fine sieve, discarding the vegetables. Reserve 2¹/2 cups of the broth for the potpie filling. Shred the chicken into bite-size pieces, discarding the skin and bones.

For the pastry, combine the flour, salt and butter in a food processor. Pulse 5 times or just until combined. Add the shortening and pulse 2 or 3 more times or until crumbly. Remove to a bowl. Add the water 1 tablespoon at a time, mixing with a fork until the mixture forms a ball. Flatten into a disk. Chill, covered in plastic wrap, for 30 minutes or for up to 2 days before rolling.

TIP: It calls for potpie tins or ramekins for serving.

For the filling, melt the butter in a large saucepan over medium heat. Add the onion, carrots and celery and cook for 10 minutes or until the onion is soft and translucent, stirring occasionally. Add the flour and cook for 1 minute, stirring constantly. Whisk in the milk and reserved chicken broth gradually. Reduce the heat to low and simmer for 10 minutes, stirring frequently. Add the chicken, thyme, sherry, peas, parsley, salt and pepper and mix well. Taste and adjust the seasonings. Divide the warm filling among six 10- to 12-ounce potpie tins or individual ramekins.

To assemble, roll the pastry $1/4$ inch thick on a floured surface. Cut into rounds about 1 inch larger than each dish's circumference. Lay a pastry round over each potpie. Tuck the overhanging pastry back under itself and press the edges with a fork to seal. Cut a 1-inch slit in the top of each pie. Beat the egg and water together and brush some of the mixture over each potpie. Place the potpies on a baking sheet covered with foil. Bake in a preheated 400-degree oven for 25 minutes or until the pastry is golden and the filling is bubbling.

Yield: 6 servings

MARSHALL FIELD'S WALNUT ROOM

Mrs. Hering's Famous Chicken Potpie is more than the most requested item on the Walnut Room's menu; it's the soul of Marshall Field's culinary history. The potpie's humble introduction to Marshall Field's guests by Mrs. Hering in 1890 resulted in the opening of the famed Walnut Room, the very first restaurant in a department store.

While the name has been changed to Macy's, the Walnut Room remains a favorite among Chicagoans.

Beef Tenderloin with Merlot Shallot Sauce

1 (6-pound) beef tenderloin,
trimmed of silver skin
Melted butter
Pepper to taste
Merlot Shallot Sauce (at right)

Let the beef tenderloin stand at room temperature for 3 to 4 hours before roasting. Place on a rack in a roasting pan. Brush with melted butter and season with pepper. Bake at 425 degrees (the oven does not have to be preheated) for 45 to 60 minutes or to 130 to 135 degrees on a meat thermometer for rare or to 140 degrees for medium-rare. Let stand for 15 minutes. The meat will continue to cook while standing.

Slice and serve with Merlot Shallot Sauce.

Yield: 8 servings

FROM ELIZABETH'S KITCHEN

I received this recipe from Mrs. Bransford (Jeanne) Whitlow, our next-door neighbor in Jackson, Tennessee. She was a very grand and fun-loving lady and a fabulous hostess. She was always beautifully dressed and had exquisite jewelry. As a child in the early years of the twentieth century, she waltzed with the Prince of Wales on an Atlantic Ocean crossing on the *Queen Mary*. My sisters and I called her Miss Jeanne.

—Elizabeth Hurley

Merlot Shallot Sauce

$1/3$ cup finely chopped shallots
$1 1/2$ cups merlot
$1 1/2$ cups beef broth
1 teaspoon butter
3 tablespoons chopped fresh parsley
$1/4$ teaspoon kosher salt

Sauté the shallots in a greased skillet for 3 minutes or until tender. Stir in the merlot. Bring to a boil and reduce the heat. Simmer for 4 minutes or until reduced to $3/4$ cup. Stir in the beef broth. Simmer for 6 minutes or until reduced to $1 1/4$ cups. Add the butter and stir until melted. Add the parsley and salt.

Serve with roast tenderloin.

Yield: $1 1/4$ cups sauce

Spicy Beef Ribs

6 tablespoons butter, softened
1 tablespoon Worcestershire sauce
2 teaspoons curry powder or cumin powder
1 teaspoon dry mustard
1/2 to 1 teaspoon freshly ground black pepper
Cayenne pepper to taste
1/2 teaspoon kosher salt
2 1/2 to 3 pounds lean beef back ribs
1/2 cup all-purpose flour
1/2 teaspoon kosher salt

Spread 2 tablespoons of the butter in a roasting pan. Cream the remaining 4 tablespoons butter with the Worcestershire sauce, curry powder, dry mustard, black pepper, cayenne pepper and 1/2 teaspoon salt in a small bowl. Coat the ribs with the flour, shaking off any excess. Sprinkle with 1/2 teaspoon salt. Roast fat side up in a preheated 450-degree oven for 10 minutes. Brush the butter mixture over the ribs. Reduce the heat to 400 degrees. Roast for 30 to 35 minutes longer or until tender.

Yield: 4 servings

Steak and Spinach Pinwheels

8 slices bacon, cooked as noted below
1 to 1 1/2 pounds flank steak, scored across the grain
Salt and pepper to taste
1 (10-ounce) package frozen chopped spinach, thawed and squeezed dry
1/4 cup grated Parmesan cheese
1/2 teaspoon minced garlic
Wooden picks
Skewers

Cook the bacon in a skillet just until done but not crisp; drain. Pound the flank steak into an 8×12-inch rectangle, working from the center to the edges. Sprinkle with salt and pepper. Layer the bacon strips lengthwise over the steak. Spread the spinach over the bacon and sprinkle with the cheese and garlic. Roll up from the short side and secure with wooden picks at 1-inch intervals, beginning 1/2 inch from one end. Cut the meat roll between the wooden picks into eight 1-inch slices. Thread 2 slices onto each of four skewers. Grill for 6 minutes. Turn and continue to grill until desired degree of doneness. Remove the wooden picks before serving.

Yield: 3 to 4 servings

Cocoa-Crusted Venison Strip Loin with White Chocolate Chestnut Purée, Brussels Sprouts and a Semisweet Venison Reduction

This recipe was contributed by the Executive Chef of The Pump Room.

Some ingredients just go hand in hand: venison and chocolate are great examples, although the combination is somewhat underestimated. Cocoa nibs give the venison a slightly bitter and cocoa finish. The chocolate brings down the gaminess of the venison and makes it more approachable.

CHOCOLATE CHESTNUT PURÉE
4 ounces frozen or dried chestnuts
(soak the dried ones in
water until soft)
$1/4$ yellow onion, sliced
1 garlic clove, crushed
Vegetable oil for cooking
$1/2$ vanilla bean, scraped
1 cup (or more) chicken stock,
vegetable stock, beef stock or water
1 tablespoon cold butter
1 tablespoon crème fraîche or cream
2 ounces white chocolate, chopped
Salt to taste

VENISON SAUCE
2 tablespoons vegetable oil
1 pound venison or beef stew meat
$3/4$ yellow onion, sliced
8 garlic cloves, crushed
$1/2$ cup (1 stick) butter
8 ounces red wine (such as a southern
Rhone, preferably a Syrah)
4 cups chicken stock
2 ounces semisweet chocolate, chopped

VENISON
4 (6-ounce) portions of venison
Salt and pepper to taste
$1/2$ cup cocoa nibs, pulsed slightly
in a coffee grinder
Vegetable oil for sautéing
Brussels sprouts

For the chocolate chestnut purée, sauté the chestnuts, onion and garlic in a little oil in a skillet until the onion is tender. Add the vanilla and chicken stock. Simmer for 20 minutes or until the liquid is reduced by half. Purée in a blender. Add the butter, crème fraîche and white chocolate and purée until smooth, adding more stock if the mixture is too thick. Season with salt. Place in a bowl and cover tightly with plastic wrap to prevent a skin from forming.

For the venison sauce, heat the oil in a saucepan over high heat until smoking. Add the venison and sauté until brown on all sides. Add the onion, garlic and butter. Cook for 3 minutes longer. Add the red wine. Cook to deglaze the pan, stirring constantly. Add the chicken stock. Simmer over low heat for 1 hour. Strain the sauce and return to the pan. Cook until reduced to a sauce consistency. Add the chocolate and stir until melted.

For the venison, season the venison portions with salt and pepper. Coat with the cocoa nibs. Sear the venison on both sides in a little oil in a skillet over medium heat. Place in a roasting pan. Roast in a preheated 400-degree oven for 5 to 10 minutes or to the desired degree of doneness. Let stand at room temperature for 10 minutes before serving. Sauté the brussels sprouts in a little oil in a skillet for 2 minutes. Season with salt and pepper.

To serve, spoon some of the chocolate chestnut purée onto the center of each plate. Add some of the brussels sprouts. Top with a portion of venison. Spoon the venison sauce over the top.

Yield: 4 servings

TIP: To spice it up a bit, add some chopped toasted hazelnuts
and grapes to the brussels sprouts.

A SWIZZLE OF CELERY

Using a celery stick to garnish a Bloody Mary
originated in the 1960s at Chicago's
Ambassador East Hotel. An unnamed
celebrity was served a Bloody Mary with no
swizzle stick. He grabbed a stalk of celery
from the relish tray to stir his drink and
history was made.

155

Pan-Seared Diver Scallops with Chanterelle Mushrooms in Truffle Sauce

1 1/2 teaspoons olive oil
1/2 pound fresh chanterelles
1 teaspoon minced shallots
1/4 teaspoon chopped fresh thyme
Salt and pepper to taste
12 large diver scallops
1 1/2 teaspoons olive oil
1/4 cup white wine
2 tablespoons butter
1 tablespoon finely chopped black truffle
Lemon juice
1 tomato, peeled, seeded and diced
Fresh herbs (optional)

Heat a heavy-bottomed sauté pan over medium-high heat. Add 1 1/2 teaspoons olive oil, the chanterelles, shallots and thyme. Sauté for 2 minutes or until the mushrooms are tender. Season with salt and pepper. Keep warm. Pat the scallops dry and season with salt and pepper. Sauté in 1 1/2 teaspoons olive oil in a heavy skillet over medium-high heat for 2 minutes on each side or until golden brown and done to medium-rare. Place in a dish and keep warm. Add the white wine to the skillet. Cook until the liquid is reduced to a few tablespoons. Whisk in the butter over low heat. Stir in the truffle. Season with salt, pepper and a few drops of lemon juice.

Divide the mushrooms among four plates. Top each with 3 scallops. Drizzle the sauce around the scallops and sprinkle with the tomato. Garnish with fresh herbs.

Yield: 4 servings

Spinach Lasagna

1 cup chopped fresh mushrooms
1 onion, chopped
1 tablespoon minced garlic
2 tablespoons olive oil
6 cups fresh spinach, chopped
32 ounces ricotta cheese
2/3 cup grated Romano cheese
1 egg
1 teaspoon basil
1 teaspoon oregano
1 teaspoon salt
1/2 teaspoon pepper
2 large jars chunky garden pasta sauce
12 no-cook lasagna noodles
3 to 4 cups (12 to 16 ounces) shredded
mozzarella cheese
1 cup freshly grated Parmesan cheese

Sauté the mushrooms, onion and garlic in the olive oil in a skillet over medium-high heat until the onion is tender. Drain off the excess liquid and let the mushroom mixture cool. Combine the spinach, ricotta cheese, Romano cheese, egg, basil, oregano, salt and pepper in a mixing bowl. Add the mushroom mixture. Beat at low speed for 1 minute. Spread 1/2 jar of the pasta sauce in a 9×13-inch lasagna pan. Layer 4 lasagna noodles, 2 cups of the spinach mixture, 1 cup mozzarella cheese, 1/3 cup Parmesan cheese and 1/2 jar of the pasta sauce over the top. Repeat the layers two times, ending with the Parmesan cheese. Bake, covered with foil, in a preheated 350-degree oven for 1 hour. Bake, uncovered, for 10 to 15 minutes longer if the lasagna looks too "soupy." Cool for 15 minutes before serving.

Yield: 8 servings

Penne with Tomato, Cream and Five Cheeses

2 cups heavy whipping cream
1 cup chopped drained canned tomatoes
1 (10-ounce) can heavy tomato purée
1/2 cup freshly grated Romano cheese
1/2 cup (2 ounces) coarsely shredded fontina cheese
4 teaspoons crumbled Gorgonzola cheese
2 tablespoons ricotta cheese
1 (6-ounce) package mozzarella cheese, cut into slices
6 fresh basil leaves, chopped, or
    1 tablespoon dried basil
1 pound uncooked bow-tie pasta
5 quarts water
Salt to taste
4 tablespoons butter, chopped

Combine the cream, tomatoes, tomato purée, Romano cheese, fontina cheese, Gorgonzola cheese, ricotta cheese, mozzarella cheese and basil in a large bowl and mix well. Cook the pasta in 5 quarts boiling salted water for 11 minutes; drain. Toss with the cheese mixture. Pour into a large baking dish. Dot with the butter. Bake in a preheated 450-degree oven for 7 to 15 minutes or until bubbly.

Yield: 6 servings

Roasted Asparagus with Balsamic Browned Butter

40 asparagus spears, trimmed
(about 2 pounds)
2 teaspoons olive oil
1/4 teaspoon kosher salt
1/8 teaspoon pepper
2 tablespoons butter
2 teaspoons soy sauce
1 teaspoon balsamic vinegar

Arrange the asparagus in a singe layer on a baking sheet. Drizzle with the olive oil and toss to coat evenly. Sprinkle with the salt and pepper. Bake in a preheated 400-degree oven for 12 minutes or until tender. Place in a serving dish. Melt the butter in a small skillet over medium heat. Cook for 3 minutes or until lightly browned, shaking the pan occasionally. Remove from the heat. Stir in the soy sauce and vinegar. Drizzle over the asparagus and toss to coat. Serve immediately.

Yield: 8 servings

Sweet Potato Casserole

1 large can sweet potatoes
3/4 cup granulated sugar
3 eggs
1 teaspoon vanilla extract
1/4 teaspoon salt
1/2 cup (1 stick) butter, melted
1 cup packed brown sugar
Chopped pecans
Shredded coconut to taste

Combine the sweet potatoes, granulated sugar, eggs, vanilla and salt in a mixing bowl and beat until smooth. Spread evenly in a baking dish. Combine the butter, brown sugar, pecans and coconut in a bowl and mix well. Spread over the sweet potato mixture. Bake in a preheated 350-degree oven for 45 minutes.

Yield: 8 to 10 servings

Baked Risotto with Asparagus, Spinach and Parmesan

1 cup finely chopped onion
1 tablespoon olive oil
1 cup uncooked arborio rice
8 cups spinach leaves (about 4 ounces)
2 cups chicken broth
1/4 teaspoon salt
1/4 teaspoon nutmeg
1/4 cup freshly grated Parmesan cheese
1 1/2 cups diagonally sliced asparagus (1-inch pieces)
1/4 cup freshly grated Parmesan cheese

Sauté the onion in the olive oil in a Dutch oven over medium heat for 4 minutes or until tender. Add the rice and mix well. Stir in the spinach, chicken broth, salt and nutmeg. Bring to a boil. Reduce the heat and simmer for 7 minutes. Stir in 1/4 cup cheese. Bake, covered, in a preheated 400-degree oven for 15 minutes. Stir in the asparagus. Sprinkle 1/4 cup cheese over the top. Bake, covered, for 10 to 15 minutes longer or until the liquid is almost absorbed.

Yield: 4 servings

TIP: A Dutch oven is a thick-walled, cast-iron cooking
pot with a tight-fitting lid.

Mashed Potato Casserole

2 pounds baking potatoes, peeled and
cut into 1-inch pieces
Salt to taste
8 ounces cream cheese
1 cup plain yogurt
1/2 teaspoon garlic powder
1/2 teaspoon salt
2 tablespoons butter, melted
1/2 teaspoon paprika

Simmer the potatoes in boiling salted water to cover in a saucepan for 20 minutes or until very tender; drain. Combine the potatoes, cream cheese, yogurt, garlic powder and 1/2 teaspoon salt in a mixing bowl. Beat at medium speed for 2 minutes or until smooth. Spoon into a greased 7×11-inch baking dish. Drizzle with the butter and sprinkle with the paprika. Bake in a preheated 350-degree oven for 30 minutes or until heated through. Cool to room temperature before serving.

Yield: 7 servings

TIP: Try leaving the potato skins on to add texture and
color to this casserole recipe.

POTATOES AND PARSNIPS

Try substituting parsnips
for half of the potatoes in
your favorite mashed potato recipe. Peel and
dice the parsnips as you would a potato and
boil for half as long.

Cream Cheese Brownies

BROWNIES
1/2 cup (1 stick) butter, softened
1 1/2 cups sugar
1 teaspoon vanilla extract
2 egg whites
1 egg
2/3 cup baking cocoa
1/2 cup milk
1 1/2 cups all-purpose flour
1/2 teaspoon baking powder
1/4 teaspoon salt

TOPPING
8 ounces cream cheese, softened
1 tablespoon cornstarch
1 teaspoon vanilla extract
1 (14-ounce) can sweetened
  condensed milk
1 egg

For the brownies, cream the butter at medium speed in a mixing bowl until fluffy. Add the sugar and vanilla. Beat for 5 minutes or until light and fluffy. Add the egg whites and egg one at a time, mixing well after each addition. Beat in the baking cocoa and milk. Combine the flour, baking powder and salt in a bowl. Add to the creamed mixture, beating just until blended. Spoon into a greased 9×13-inch baking pan.

For the topping, beat the cream cheese at medium speed in a mixing bowl until smooth. Add the cornstarch, vanilla, condensed milk and egg in the order given, beating well after each addition. Spread evenly over the chocolate mixture. Bake in a preheated 350-degree oven for 30 to 35 minutes or until set. Cool in the pan on a wire rack.

Yield: 36 brownies

Double Chocolate Cookies with Dried Cherries

1 1/4 cups all-purpose flour
1/2 teaspoon baking powder
1/4 teaspoon salt
5 tablespoons butter, softened
1/2 cup granulated sugar
1/2 cup packed brown sugar
1 egg
1 1/2 teaspoons vanilla extract
2/3 cup dried tart cherries
3/4 cup semisweet chocolate chunks
3/4 cup premium white chocolate chips

Whisk the flour, baking powder and salt together in a small bowl. Cream the butter, granulated sugar and brown sugar in a mixing bowl until light and fluffy. Add the egg and vanilla. Beat for 1 minute longer. Add the flour mixture and mix well. Stir in the cherries, chocolate chunks and white chocolate chips. Drop by level teaspoonfuls 2 inches apart onto a cookie sheet. Place the cookie sheet in the freezer for 5 minutes. Bake in a preheated 350-degree oven for 10 to 12 minutes or until lightly browned. Cool on the cookie sheet for 2 minutes. Place on a wire rack to cool completely.

Yield: 24 cookies

TIP: Add baking cocoa to the batter, omit the chocolate chunks, increase the white chocolate chips to 1 cup, and double the amount of cherries.

THE JUNIOR LEAGUE'S HOLIDAY SHOPPING GAZEBO

For the past thirty-six years, the Junior League of Chicago has helped kick off the season by hosting an annual Holiday Shopping Gazebo. It's the ultimate gift-with-purchase shopping event and is hosted at a variety of venues throughout the city. There is always a pre-party, and the vendors delight with rare finds that make the perfect gift for everyone on your list. Join us this year and celebrate the season with this almond fudge, named in honor of one of our longest running events.

Junior League of Chicago's Gazebo Almond Fudge

1 (8-ounce) can almond paste
1 cup whole milk
1 cup sugar
6 tablespoons butter, softened

Combine the almond paste, milk, sugar and 2 tablespoons of the butter in a large skillet over high heat, stirring and mashing with the back of a wooden spoon. Bring to a boil. Reduce the heat to low. Cook for 25 minutes, stirring occasionally. The mixture will thicken as the liquid cooks off. Cut the remaining 4 tablespoons butter into chunks. Add to the pan. Cook, stirring constantly, until a paste forms and the swirls formed by the stirring remain visible. Turn off the heat if necessary to prevent scorching. Spread evenly in a foil-lined baking pan. Refrigerate for 1 hour or until firm. Invert onto a cutting board and peel off the foil. Cut into 1/2-inch squares. Store in the refrigerator.

Yield: 12 servings

TIP: Add chopped nuts and/or chocolate for chocolate lovers.

Holiday Bark

Saltines
1 cup (2 sticks) butter
1 cup packed brown sugar
12 ounces semisweet chocolate chips
Finely chopped walnuts (optional)

Line a rectangular baking pan with foil; butter the foil thoroughly, including the corners and sides. Cover the bottom of the pan with a layer of saltines. Melt the butter with the brown sugar in a saucepan over high heat, stirring constantly. Bring to a boil. Pour evenly over the saltines. Bake in a preheated 350-degree oven for 10 minutes. Pour the chocolate chips over the bubbling brown sugar mixture. Let the chocolate melt for a few seconds; spread evenly over the brown sugar mixture. Sprinkle with the walnuts. Place in the freezer until firm. Break into pieces and store in an airtight container in the refrigerator.

Yield: 12 servings

TIP: If nut allergies are a problem, substitute chopped M&M candies for the walnuts.

Scotch Bars

1 cup graham cracker crumbs
2/3 cup packed brown sugar
1/2 cup all-purpose flour
1/3 cup quick-cooking oats
1/3 cup butterscotch morsels
1 teaspoon baking powder
1 tablespoon vegetable oil
1 1/2 teaspoons vanilla extract
2 egg whites
1 tablespoon confectioners' sugar

Combine the graham cracker crumbs, brown sugar, flour, oats, butterscotch morsels and baking powder in a large bowl and mix well. Whisk the oil, vanilla and egg whites together in a small bowl. Add to the dry ingredients and stir just until mixed. Press into a greased 8×8-inch baking pan. Bake in a preheated 350-degree oven for 18 minutes or until a wooden pick inserted in the center comes out clean. Cool in the pan on a wire rack. Sift the confectioners' sugar over the top. Cut into bars.

Yield: 16 bars

Toffee Bars

These are a favorite of Junior League of Chicago members.

1/2 cup (1 stick) butter
1 1/2 cups graham cracker crumbs
1 (14-ounce) can sweetened condensed milk
1 1/4 cups almond toffee bits (1 package)
1 1/4 cups English toffee bits (1 package)
6 ounces semisweet chocolate chips
1 cup chopped pecans
1/2 cup sliced almonds

Melt the butter in a 9×13-inch baking dish in a preheated 325-degree oven. Layer the graham cracker crumbs, condensed milk, almond toffee bits, English toffee bits, chocolate chips, pecans and almonds over the butter. Press the layers firmly. Bake for 25 minutes or until the edges are lightly browned. Cool on a wire rack. Cut into bars.

Yield: 24 bars

Iced Sugar Cookies

COOKIES
1 1/2 cups confectioners' sugar
1/2 cup (1 stick) margarine, softened
1/2 cup (1 stick) butter, softened
1 egg
1 teaspoon vanilla extract
1/2 teaspoon almond extract
2 1/2 cups all-purpose flour
1 teaspoon baking soda
1 teaspoon cream of tartar

VANILLA ICING
1 cup confectioners' sugar
2 tablespoons margarine, melted
1 teaspoon vanilla extract
1 to 2 tablespoons hot water

For the cookies, cream the confectioners' sugar, margarine and butter in a mixing bowl until light and fluffy. Beat in the egg, vanilla and almond extract. Combine the flour, baking soda and cream of tartar in a bowl. Add to the creamed mixture and mix well. Shape into a ball. Chill, covered with plastic wrap, for 1 hour or more. Roll 1/8 inch thick on a surface sprinkled with confectioners' sugar. Cut into shapes with a cookie cutter. Bake on a cookie sheet in a preheated 375-degree oven for 8 to 10 minutes. Cool on a wire rack.

For the icing, combine the confectioners' sugar and margarine in a small bowl. Add the vanilla and enough hot water to make of thin consistency. Drizzle over the cooled cookies.

Yield: 24 cookies

Chocolate Gingerbread Cookies

1¹/₂ cups plus 1 tablespoon all-purpose flour
1 tablespoon baking cocoa
1 teaspoon ground ginger
1 teaspoon cinnamon
¹/₄ teaspoon ground cloves
¹/₄ teaspoon nutmeg
¹/₂ cup (1 stick) butter, softened
³/₄ tablespoon grated fresh ginger
¹/₂ cup packed dark brown sugar
¹/₂ cup unsulfured molasses
1 teaspoon baking soda
1¹/₂ teaspoons boiling water
7 ounces semisweet chocolate chips
¹/₄ cup granulated sugar

Sift the flour, baking cocoa, ground ginger, cinnamon, cloves and nutmeg together into a bowl. Cream the butter with the grated ginger in a mixing bowl for 4 minutes. Add the brown sugar and beat until smooth. Beat in the molasses. Dissolve the baking soda in the boiling water in a small bowl. Add ¹/₂ of the flour mixture to the molasses mixture and mix well. Beat in the baking soda mixture. Add the remaining flour mixture and mix well. Stir in the chocolate chips. Pat the dough 1 inch thick on a piece of plastic wrap. Wrap tightly and chill in the refrigerator for 2 hours.

Shape the dough into 1¹/₂-inch balls. Place 2 inches apart on a nonstick cookie sheet. Chill in the refrigerator for 20 minutes. Roll the balls in the granulated sugar. Bake in a preheated 325-degree oven for 10 to 12 minutes or until the surface cracks. Cool on the cookie sheet for 5 minutes. Remove to a wire rack to cool completely.

Yield: 3 dozen cookies

Lemon Ginger Cookies

³/₄ cup (1¹/₂ sticks) butter, softened
1¹/₂ cups packed brown sugar
¹/₄ cup molasses
1 egg
5¹/₂ cups all-purpose flour
2 to 3 tablespoons freshly grated lemon zest
2 teaspoons baking soda
1 tablespoon ginger
1 teaspoon cinnamon
¹/₂ teaspoon salt
¹/₃ cup granulated sugar

Cream the butter and brown sugar in a mixing bowl until light and fluffy. Add the molasses and egg and beat until smooth. Combine the flour, lemon zest, baking soda, ginger, cinnamon and salt in a bowl. Add to the creamed mixture and beat until smooth. Shape into 1-inch balls. Roll the balls in the granulated sugar. Bake on an ungreased cookie sheet in a preheated 350-degree oven for 10 minutes. The cookies will still be soft in the center. Cool on a wire rack.

Yield: 30 cookies

Snow Balls

These cookies are just as delicious with walnuts instead of pecans.

1 cup (2 sticks) butter, softened
1/2 cup sugar
2 cups all-purpose flour
2 cups finely chopped pecans
1 tablespoon vanilla extract
Confectioners' sugar

Cream the butter and sugar in a mixing bowl until light and fluffy. Beat in the flour, pecans and vanilla. Shape by tablespoonfuls into balls. Bake on an ungreased cookie sheet in a preheated 350-degree oven for 12 to 15 minutes. Coat the warm cookies with confectioners' sugar. Cool on a wire rack. Coat again with confectioners' sugar.

Yield: 4 dozen cookies

Frango Mint Chocolate Cookies

This recipe was provided by Marshall Field's.

1 cup (2 sticks) unsalted butter, softened
1/2 cup confectioners' sugar
2 cups cake flour
1 teaspoon vanilla extract
1/8 teaspoon salt
1 cup finely chopped pecans
18 Frango Mint chocolates, cut vertically into halves
Confectioners' sugar for sprinkling

Cream the butter and 1/2 cup confectioners' sugar in a bowl for 1 minute or until light and fluffy. Add the flour, vanilla and salt and stir with a wooden spoon until combined. Stir in the pecans. Chill, loosely covered with plastic wrap, for 1 hour or until the dough is firm. Shape 1 tablespoon dough around each chocolate half, forming a ball. Place 1 inch apart on two nonstick cookie sheets. Bake one cookie sheet on the top rack and one on the center rack in a preheated 350-degree oven for 10 minutes. Switch the cookie sheets. Bake for 8 to 10 minutes or until golden brown. Sift confectioners' sugar generously over the cookies. Cool on a wire rack.

Yield: 3 dozen cookies

Frosted Brownies

BROWNIES
1/2 cup (1 stick) butter or margarine, softened
1 cup sugar
4 eggs
1 teaspoon vanilla extract
1 (1-pound) can Hershey's chocolate syrup
1 cup plus 1 tablespoon sifted all-purpose flour
1/2 teaspoon baking powder
1/2 teaspoon salt

CHOCOLATE FROSTING
1/2 cup (1 stick) butter or margarine
1 1/2 cups sugar
1/3 cup evaporated milk
3 ounces semisweet chocolate chips

For the brownies, cream the butter and sugar in a bowl until light and fluffy. Add the eggs two at a time and the vanilla, beating well after each addition. Stir in the chocolate syrup. Sift the flour, baking powder and salt together and stir into the creamed mixture. Pour into a greased 9×13-inch baking pan. Bake in a preheated 350-degree oven for 20 to 25 minutes. Cool in the pan on a wire rack.

For the frosting, combine the butter, sugar, evaporated milk and chocolate chips in a saucepan. Bring to a boil and boil for 1 minute, being careful not to burn. Add the chocolate chips and stir until melted. Beat until beginning to thicken. Pour over the brownies (the frosting should still be hot so that it spreads itself). Cut into bars.

Yield: 16 brownies

Hazelnut Gâteau

4 egg whites
Pinch of salt
1/4 teaspoon cream of tartar
1 cup superfine sugar
1/4 cup finely chopped hazelnuts

2 (13-ounce) jars hazelnut
  cocoa spread (such as Nutella)
2 tablespoons chopped hazelnuts
1 tablespoon confectioners' sugar

Beat the egg whites with a pinch of salt in a mixing bowl until soft peaks form. Beat in the cream of tartar. Add 3/4 cup of the superfine sugar 1 tablespoon at a time, beating until stiff peaks form. Fold in the remaining 1/4 cup superfine sugar and 1/4 cup chopped hazelnuts. Spread the batter into 8-inch rounds on four baking parchment-lined baking sheets. Bake the rounds in two preheated 245-degree ovens (two baking sheets in each oven) for 1 hour or until dry. Cool on a wire rack. Spoon the hazelnut cocoa spread into a microwave-safe dish. Microwave until warm enough to stir easily; cool slightly. Spread between the meringue layers and over the top. Sprinkle with 2 tablespoons hazelnuts and the confectioners' sugar. Let stand, covered with a cake dome, at room temperature for 12 to 24 hours before serving.

Yield: 8 to 10 servings

TIP: The use of two ovens is essential in this recipe. The meringue rounds need plenty of air circulation to bake properly. It is also important to make this dessert twelve to twenty-four hours before serving and let it rest under a cake dome to settle and firm up.

FROM ELIZABETH'S KITCHEN

My mom made this recipe every Christmas for many years. However, she made a homemade chocolate filling using egg yolks, and it curdled easily. I adapted the recipe by using hazelnut cocoa spread and just heating it in the microwave. I love this recipe for parties because you have to make it the morning of or the night before the party. It forces you to get one more thing off your checklist! —Elizabeth Hurley

Cinnamon Cheesecake Squares

2 (10-ounce) cans crescent roll dough
16 ounces cream cheese, softened
1 cup sugar
1 teaspoon vanilla extract
$1/2$ cup (1 stick) butter, melted
$1/2$ cup sugar
1 teaspoon cinnamon

Unroll 1 can crescent roll dough. Press onto the bottom of an ungreased 9×13-inch baking pan. Beat the cream cheese, 1 cup sugar and the vanilla in a bowl until smooth. Spread over the dough. Unroll the second can of crescent roll dough. Press over the cream cheese mixture, stretching to cover completely. Pour the butter over the top. Mix $1/2$ cup sugar and the cinnamon in a small bowl and sprinkle over the butter. Bake in a preheated 350-degree oven for 30 minutes. Cool completely before cutting into squares.

Serve warm with vanilla ice cream and sliced apples.

Yield: 10 to 12 servings

Chocolate Chip Pie

2 eggs
$1/2$ cup packed brown sugar
$1/2$ cup granulated sugar
1 teaspoon vanilla extract
$1/2$ cup all-purpose flour
$1/8$ teaspoon salt
$1/2$ cup (1 stick) butter, melted
6 ounces semisweet chocolate chips
1 cup chopped walnuts
1 unbaked (9-inch) deep-dish pie shell

Whisk the eggs, brown sugar, granulated sugar and vanilla together in a large bowl. Beat in the flour and salt. Whisk in the butter $1/3$ at a time. Stir in the chocolate chips and walnuts. Pour into the pie shell. Bake in a preheated 325-degree oven for 50 minutes or until puffed and golden brown. Cool on a rack for 30 minutes. Serve warm or at room temperature.

Yield: 8 servings

Rich and Delicious Dessert

1 (2-layer) package yellow cake mix
1/2 cup (1 stick) butter, softened
2 eggs
12 ounces semisweet chocolate chips
6 ounces chopped toffee bits
6 ounces white chocolate chips
32 caramels
1/2 cup (1 stick) butter
1 (14-ounce) can sweetened condensed milk

Combine the cake mix, butter and eggs in a mixing bowl and mix until crumbly. Stir in the semisweet chocolate chips, toffee bits and white chocolate chips. Press 1/2 of the dough into a greased 9×13-inch baking pan. Bake in a preheated 350-degree oven for 10 to 12 minutes. Combine the caramels, butter and condensed milk in a saucepan. Cook over low heat until melted and smooth, stirring constantly. Pour slowly over the crust, avoiding the edges. Crumble the remaining dough over the caramel mixture. Bake in a preheated 350-degree oven for 20 minutes or until set. Cool for 20 to 30 minutes. Run a knife blade around the edges of the pan. Cool for 40 minutes longer before cutting. Cut into very small pieces.

Yield: 24 servings

ALL ABOUT CHOCOLATE

The higher the percentage of cocoa contained in a chocolate, the less sweet it will be.
Here are the basic types:

UNSWEETENED CHOCOLATE, also known as bitter or baking chocolate, is unadulterated chocolate liquor. The pure, ground, roasted cocoa beans impart a strong, deep chocolate flavor. With the addition of sugar, however, it is used as the base for cakes, brownies, confections, and cookies.

DARK CHOCOLATE is chocolate without milk as an additive.

MILK CHOCOLATE is chocolate with milk powder or condensed milk added.

SEMISWEET CHOCOLATE is often used for cooking purposes. It is dark chocolate with a high sugar content.

BITTERSWEET CHOCOLATE is chocolate liquor (or unsweetened chocolate) to which sugar, more cocoa butter, lecithin, and vanilla have been added. It has less sugar and more liquor than semisweet chocolate, but the two are interchangeable in baking.

WHITE CHOCOLATE is a confection based on cocoa butter without the cocoa solids.

"FIRST HUSBANDS CLUB"

A time-honored tradition of the Junior League of Chicago, the "First Husbands Club" gathers for an annual dinner

to welcome their newest member. The men are bound by a shared understanding of what it means for a wife

to serve as the JLC President. Over dinner, the veteran husbands give the rookie pointers for surviving the busy year.

All the men prepare a signature dish for the dinner, and they were kind enough to share some of their favorites with us.

We think you'll find them quite delicious!

FIRST HUSBAND MEMBERS

Vern Broders • Paul Bodine • Tim Snyder • Mark Hurley • Jeff Kerr

Honorary mascot
Beau Snyder (dog)

Beef Rolled in Lettuce Wraps

Submitted by Jeff Kerr

1 pound ground beef
1 tablespoon vegetable oil
1 carrot, diced
2 ribs celery, diced
6 green onions, chopped
1 can water chestnuts, drained
1 tablespoon vegetable oil
1/4 cup hoisin sauce
1 tablespoon soy sauce
1/4 teaspoon freshly ground pepper
2 tablespoons cornstarch
1/4 cup chicken broth
Lettuce leaves

Brown the ground beef in 1 tablespoon oil in a skillet, stirring until crumbly; drain. Sauté the carrot, celery, green onions and water chestnuts in 1 tablespoon oil in another skillet for 3 minutes. Add to the browned beef. Stir in the hoisin sauce, soy sauce and pepper. Cook for 1 minute, stirring constantly. Dissolve the cornstarch in the chicken broth and add to the beef mixture. Cook until thickened, stirring constantly. Spoon 1 or 2 tablespoons of the beef mixture onto each lettuce leaf. Roll up and serve.

Yield: 4 servings

CARRYOVER COOKING

The internal temperature of the food continues to rise after it is removed from the oven, and this can change the degree of doneness. The larger the item, the greater the amount of heat it will retain. Therefore, items should be removed from the oven when the internal temperature is lower than the desired service temperature.

"Don't Tell Peggy" Secret Meat Loaf

Submitted by Paul Bodine

This is a recipe for the guys to make when she's out for the evening at the Junior League. (Don't let her discover that you know how to cook!)

2 pounds ground chuck
1 cup unflavored croutons or stuffing mix
1 cup frozen corn kernels
2 eggs, beaten
1 tablespoon Worcestershire sauce
1/2 teaspoon salt
1/2 teaspoon pepper
Ketchup
2 slices bacon

Combine the ground chuck, croutons, corn, eggs, Worcestershire sauce, salt and pepper in a large bowl and mix well. Shape into a loaf in a baking dish. Press a deep lengthwise groove into the top of the loaf. Fill the groove with ketchup. Place 1 piece of bacon along either side of the groove. Bake in a preheated 350-degree oven for 1 hour for medium or 1 1/4 hours for well done.

Yield: 4 to 6 servings

Golden Garlic Mashed Potatoes

Submitted by Vern Broders

1 pound rutabagas,
peeled and cut into 1-inch chunks
3 pounds Yukon Gold potatoes,
peeled and cut into 2-inch chunks
5 garlic cloves
1/2 cup skim milk
1/2 cup (1 stick) margarine
1 cup plain yogurt, at room temperature
1/2 cup grated Parmesan cheese
1 tablespoon horseradish
3 tablespoons chives
2 teaspoons salt
1/2 teaspoon pepper
1/4 teaspoon nutmeg

Cook the rutabagas in a large pot filled with boiling water for 15 minutes. Add the potatoes and garlic to the water. Simmer, covered, for 20 minutes or until the potatoes are tender. Drain in a colander and return the vegetables to the pot. Add the skim milk and margarine and mash just until lumpy. Add the yogurt and mash until smooth. Stir in the cheese, horseradish, chives, salt, pepper and nutmeg.

Yield: 10 servings

A NOTE FROM MARK

"Cheese grits have been a staple in my family's cuisine for generations. They appear on the menu for every important occasion in our lives—wedding brunches, Christmas dinners, funeral visits, and so forth—and they appear frequently in the daily breakfast, lunch, and dinner rotation. Cheese grits are the closest thing we have to a true family recipe that has been handed down and modified from mother to sister to daughter to son. My mother used slightly different ingredients in her recipe, which we had to modify as newlyweds in Chicago when we couldn't get the right Kraft cheese product. We've also left out the cup of crushed and buttered cornflakes she used as a topping. The freshly baked slightly browned grits are so beautiful coming out of the oven that we didn't think they needed this adornment. Elizabeth and I enjoy serving this dish, so familiar to us, to our Yankee friends, who find them an exotic delicacy."

—Mark Hurley

Best Cheese Grits

Submitted by Mark Hurley

1 cup grits (not instant or quick-cooking)
4 cups water
1 teaspoon garlic salt
2 cups (8 ounces) shredded Cheddar cheese
1/4 cup (1/2 stick) butter, softened
3 eggs
1/2 cup milk
1 cup sour cream

Cook the grits with the water and garlic salt using the package directions. Add the cheese and butter to the hot grits and stir until melted. Whisk the eggs and milk together in a bowl. Beat in the sour cream. Add slowly to the grits, stirring constantly. Pour into a greased 2-quart baking dish. Bake in a preheated 350-degree oven for 45 to 60 minutes or until set.

Yield: 4 to 6 servings

TIP: Be sure to cook the grits in a pan large enough to accommodate all the ingredients; it's easier to combine everything in one pan and pour it into the baking dish. Cook the grits until thick; too much water left in the grits will make the casserole soupy. Try the finely shredded Cheddar or combination of Cheddar and Monterey Jack cheeses. White Cheddar seems to be too oily. A shallow 8×12-inch baking dish works well; if the dish is too deep, the grits will take forever to cook.

Apulia Spaghetti

Submitted by Mark Snyder

1 (8-count) can artichoke hearts,
drained and halved
Juice of 1 lemon
1 garlic clove, halved
2 tablespoons olive oil
2 tablespoons chopped fresh parsley
2 tablespoons all-purpose flour
1 cup crème fraîche
1 cup whipping cream
Salt and pepper to taste
1 pound (or less) spaghetti, cooked
2 tablespoons grated Parmesan cheese
2 tablespoons butter

Toss the artichoke hearts with the lemon juice in a small bowl. Let stand for 10 minutes. Sauté the garlic in the olive oil in a skillet until browned. Discard the garlic. Drain the artichoke halves. Add to the skillet with the parsley. Sauté until lightly browned. Stir in the flour. Add the crème fraîche and whipping cream gradually, stirring constantly. Season with salt and pepper. Cook just until steaming but not boiling. Spread the cooked spaghetti in a baking dish. Add the artichoke mixture and toss to combine. Top with the cheese and dot with the butter. Bake in a preheated 400-degree oven for 15 minutes.

Yield: 8 to 10 servings

THE BOOT

Apulia is a region in southeastern Italy. Its southern portion forms the heel of the Italian "boot."

Honey-Roasted Brussels Sprouts

Submitted by Vern Broders

3 or 4 slices bacon, cut crosswise
into $1/2$-inch strips
2 tablespoons honey
1 tablespoon orange zest
$1/2$ teaspoon nutmeg
$1/2$ teaspoon salt
$1 1/2$ pounds brussels sprouts
(about 15 sprouts), trimmed and halved

Scatter the bacon in a large baking pan. Roast in a preheated 450-degree oven for 10 minutes or until crisp, stirring several times. Drain the bacon on paper towels. Pour the drippings into a large bowl. Whisk in the honey, orange zest, nutmeg and salt. Add the brussels sprouts and toss to combine. Spread in the roasting pan. Roast for 20 minutes, tossing twice. Sprinkle the bacon bits over the brussels sprouts. Roast for 3 to 5 minutes longer or until the sprouts are golden brown and tender.

Yield: 6 servings

Beau's Favorite Hasenpfeffer

This recipe is best when you marinate the rabbit meat overnight before cooking. You can purchase rabbit meat (generally it will be frozen) in Chicago at Paulina Market, Fox and Obel, or Treasure Island Foods. Rabbit meat is lean, white meat and may be purchased either whole or packaged as serving pieces. Buying whole rabbits assures that you get the loin meat, which runs along the back to the hind quarters.

2 cups red wine	1 cup chopped onion
1/4 cup olive oil	1 cup chopped celery
2 bay leaves	8 ounces sliced fresh mushrooms
1 tablespoon chopped fresh sage	6 slices bacon, diced
1 tablespoon chopped fresh thyme	1/2 cup all-purpose flour
1/4 teaspoon Tabasco sauce	1 tablespoon pepper
2 whole rabbits,	1 teaspoon salt
or 2 1/2 pounds rabbit pieces	1/4 cup brandy
1 tablespoon butter	2 tablespoons chopped fresh parsley
2 garlic cloves, chopped	

Combine the red wine, olive oil, bay leaves, sage, thyme and Tabasco sauce in a deep glass dish. Add the rabbit. Marinate, covered, in the refrigerator overnight. Heat the butter with the garlic in a large skillet over medium-high heat. Add the onion. Sauté for 2 minutes. Add the celery and mushrooms and sauté for 3 minutes. Cook the bacon in another large skillet until crisp; drain, leaving a little of the drippings in the skillet. Combine the flour, pepper and salt in a shallow bowl. Drain the rabbit, reserving the marinade. Coat the rabbit with the flour mixture. Brown in the bacon drippings in the skillet for 3 to 4 minutes on each side. Place the rabbit in a baking dish. Combine the reserved marinade, onion mixture, bacon, brandy and parsley in a saucepan. Bring to a boil, stirring constantly. Pour over the rabbit. Bake in a preheated 325-degree oven for 1 hour or until the meat is fork-tender.

Yield: 6 servings

Beau is the official mascot of the JLC Garden. Before he took on this role, the Garden was rumored to have a bit of a rabbit problem. Since he was named mascot, the only "hopping" happening in the Garden is from the sustainers' annual Garden Party each spring. Thanks, Beau!

First Husbands Flan

Submitted by Tim Snyder

3/4 cup sugar	3/4 cup sugar
2 1/2 cups milk	1 teaspoon vanilla extract
5 eggs	Pinch of salt

Dissolve 3/4 cup sugar in a heavy saucepan over medium heat. Cook without stirring until golden, swirling the pan occasionally. Warm an 8-inch round baking dish under running hot water; drain and dry thoroughly. Pour the caramelized sugar into the pan, tilting and swirling the pan to coat the bottom and partway up the side. Cool for 30 minutes. Heat the milk in a saucepan until lukewarm. Bring 2 quarts of water to a boil in another saucepan. Beat the eggs with 3/4 cup of the warm milk, 3/4 cup sugar, the vanilla and salt in a large bowl. Stir in the remaining milk and pour into the caramel-lined baking dish. Place in a larger pan. Add boiling water to the larger pan to a depth of 1 inch. Bake in a preheated 350-degree oven for 50 minutes or until a knife blade inserted in the center comes out clean. Cool on a wire rack for 20 to 30 minutes. Chill, tightly covered with foil. Run a knife blade between the flan and the side of the pan. Invert onto a serving plate and scoop any caramelized sugar remaining in the pan over the flan.

Yield: 8 servings

A NOTE FROM TIM

"My mother was born and raised in Uruguay, where—as in other Latin American countries—flan is a simple but tasty dessert for regular family dinners. The basic recipe consists of caramelized sugar and custard that are baked together in a water bath. You can dress up this recipe by adding seasonal berries. Allow enough time to cool and thoroughly chill the flan after it bakes."

—Tim Snyder

Best Uses for Each Variety of Onion

BOILING ONIONS	Stews, soups, compotes
CIPPOLINI ONIONS	Baked, grilled, casserole
GARLIC	Flavoring ingredient; roasted and puréed; steamed; served à la grecque or other cold preparation
LEEKS	Stews, sauces, main ingredient or flavoring
PEARL ONIONS	Boiled, pickled, brined; stews or braises
RAMPS	Stewed or sautéed
RED ONIONS	Fresh in salads, grilled, compotes, marmalades
SCALLIONS/GREEN ONIONS	Fresh as crudité, salads, in uncooked sauces
SPANISH ONIONS	Aromatic or ingredient in soups, stews, sauces, braises; basic component of mirepoix
SWEET ONIONS (Walla Walla, Vidalia, Maui)	Fresh in salads, grilled, sautéed
YELLOW ONIONS	Aromatic or ingredient in soups, stews, sauces, braises; basic component of mirepoix
WHITE ONIONS	Aromatic or ingredient in soups, stews, sauces, braises; basic component of mirepoix

To get onion or garlic smell off your hands, try rubbing your fingers on stainless steel.

To caramelize onions, sauté them in butter and oil in a nonstick pan over high heat for 5 minutes to quickly release the moisture; then cook over medium heat for 45 minutes for clear onion flavor and a yielding yet firm texture. For flavoring, add just a little light brown sugar, salt, and black pepper.

Index

For additional copies of

PEELING THE WILD ONION,

please visit our web site, www.jlchicago.org,
or telephone the Junior League of Chicago office at
312-664-4462